Narcissistic Recovery Guide

9 Steps to Recover from Emotionally Abusive & Toxic Relationships with Narcissists & Toxic People

Rowena Spring

© **Copyright Rowena Spring 2023 - All rights reserved.**

The content contained within this book may not be reproduced, duplicated or transmitted without direct written permission from the author or the publisher.

Under no circumstances will any blame or legal responsibility be held against the publisher, or author, for any damages, reparation, or monetary loss due to the information contained within this book. Either directly or indirectly. You are responsible for your own choices, actions, and results.

Legal Notice:

This book is copyright protected. This book is only for personal use. You cannot amend, distribute, sell, use, quote or paraphrase any part, or the content within this book, without the consent of the author or publisher.

Disclaimer Notice:

Please note the information contained within this document is for educational and entertainment purposes only. All effort has been executed to present accurate, up to date, and reliable, complete information. No warranties of any kind are declared or implied. Readers acknowledge that the author is not engaging in the rendering of legal, financial, medical or professional advice. The content within this book has been derived from various sources. Please consult a licensed professional before attempting any techniques outlined in this book.

By reading this document, the reader agrees that under no circumstances is the author responsible for any losses, direct or indirect, which are incurred as a result of the use of the information contained within this document, including, but not limited to, — errors, omissions, or inaccuracies.

Contents

Introduction v

Step One: Clear The Air 12
    What is Narcissism? 13
    What about Narcissistic Personality Disorder? 15
    Origin of the word "Narcissism" 17
    Signs That You're Dealing with a Narcissist/Toxic Person ... 19
    The Truth about Narcissistic Relationships 28

Step Two: Set Boundaries 35
    Why It's Important to Set Boundaries 36
    Three Parts to Setting Boundaries 42
    How to Enforce Boundaries 45
    Common Mistakes to Avoid When Setting Boundaries 49
    Forms of Abuse to Expect After Setting Boundaries 52
    When They won't Respect Your Boundaries 58

Step Three: Time For Healing 61
    Understand That Your Feelings May Linger 63
    Anticipate Complex Emotions 67
    Steps to Healing from Abuse 73
    Exercises to Heal Your Mind 78

Step Four: Break the Vicious Cycle of Narcissistic Abuse 85
    Understanding the Narcissistic Abuse Cycle 86
    The Impact of the Narcissistic Abuse Cycle 98
    How to Break Free 101

Step Five: Pump Up Your Self-Esteem & Self-Worth 105
How Narcissistic Abuse Affects Self-Esteem and Self-Worth 106
You're Not The Many Things That Your Ex (Or Others) Say About You 110
End Negative Thoughts 111
Repairing Your Self-Esteem 114
Finding Your Self-Worth 118

Step Six: Change Your Environment 121
Create New Rituals 123
Avoid Social Media 128
Avoid Negative People 131
Spend More Time With Positive People 133

Step Seven: Find Yourself Again 136
Deal with Feelings of Failure, Shame, Guilt, Self-Pity, and Depression 136
Stop Attracting Abusers 142
Practice Self-Love (The Greatest Form of Love) 144
Prioritizing Self-Care 148

Step Eight: Seek Support 151
Why You Need External Support 152
Rely on Peer Support 154
Seek Professional Help for Narcissistic Abuse Recovery 157
How to Find a Therapist 159
How to Find a Narcissistic Abuse Support Group 163

Step Nine: On The Road To Recovery After A Toxic Relationship 166
Signs That You Are Recovering From Abuse 167
People to Be Wary of When On a Date 171
Steps To Ensure Abuse Doesn't Happen Again 175
Build Trust and Strengthen Future Relationships without Allowing Past Abuse to Affect Your Happiness 177

Conclusion 180

Resources List 183

Introduction

"Do not look for healing at the feet of those who broke you."

- Rupi Kaur

Love is calm, not chaotic!

Have you been constantly lied to, abused, manipulated, felt powerless, neglected, hopeless, confused, and your opinion never matters?

As you already know, nothing is calm about being in a relationship with a toxic person or a narcissist. With them, you probably have been manipulated, gaslighted, abused, talked down on, shamed, and made to believe that all the bad things that happened in the relationship were your fault – just to mention a few of the hurtful things narcissists can make you go through.

Being in a relationship with a narcissist can be quite physically, mentally, and emotionally draining; they sap your energy and leave you wondering what happened, struggling to know who you are, making you think you are to blame for everything, and left traumatized. Many victims of narcissistic relationships claim that their experience felt like they were in a vicious cycle where they felt stuck and didn't know how to set themselves free from the shackles of abuse.

When you're with a toxic person like a narcissist, you will struggle with self-esteem and feel inadequate. Although it won't come as a surprise to feel this way since you've completely devoted yourself to them and care less about your own feelings.

Setting goals and achieving them will likely be impossible since the narcissist will always talk down on you and make you feel worthless. You will fail to recognize your strengths and focus more on your weaknesses. They will make you believe everything should be about them, the world should revolve around them, and they are in control of your life. You will be silently bottling your pains and suffering until they burst at the seams.

While these are extremely difficult feelings to deal with, it's possible to be empowered to leave a narcissist and heal from the pain they have caused you. Regardless of your relationship with a narcissist or the type of abuse you were exposed to, you can heal and regain control of your life after ending the relationship.

When you can take the big step of setting yourself free, you can rebalance your life, prioritize your needs, love yourself more, stop walking around feeling like a burden, achieve your goals, and finally, enjoy life! Won't this be a good feeling? Of course, it is! We all want to live on our terms and be proud of ourselves as we watch all our dreams finally come to fruition.

But you might wonder, *"What do narcissists gain from abusing others?" "Why are there even narcissists in the first place?"*

For many years, "narcissistic abuse" has become a social media buzzword as people are more aware of the signs and identify their traits. This is partially due to the belief that narcissists have increased in the last few years. While researchers have looked into this, they aren't completely sure why narcissism is fast becoming a "pandemic," and many people now have to deal with the pain of dating a narcissist.

However, certain studies suggest that the reason for the existence of narcissistic abuse is due to the highly capitalist society we have recently, overly prioritizing people's success and achievement and seeing it as the most important and lacking empathy and genuine connection (Caligor et al., 2015).

Also, another study suggests that narcissistic traits come from childhood experience – when the abuser had relational trauma with repeated experiences leading to the individual feeling an extreme lack of self-esteem (Mosquera & Gonzalez, 2011). This makes the individual respond by shooting up their ego to extreme levels to protect their vulnerability. Regardless of the source of narcissism, it's fast-growing, and there are so many abusers around us.

As a counselor, I've helped victims of emotional, physical, and mental abuse heal from the pain caused by toxic people, especially narcissists. I provide support by helping survivors get back on their feet, regain their sanity, and become who they're meant to be.

I notice that many people who walk through my door for counseling often say things like, *"I don't know who I am anymore," "I can't recognize the person I see when I look in the mirror," "I feel numb and tired of feeling this way."* It's common to question yourself and your abilities when dating a narcissist. You'll even wonder if you are the abusive one and if the issues you're experiencing come from you. This complete loss of self is due to the tactical erosion of one's identity caused by a narcissist. This can be one of the most heartbreaking consequences you'll have to deal with after dating a narcissist.

Since confusion and self-doubt are common in abusive relationships, we must address those feelings to heal. Healing after a narcissistic abuse starts with knowing and accepting that you've been abused. When this happens, every other step can follow.

Healing from narcissistic abuse can be a tough journey – I won't be sugarcoating it. However, it will get easier over time with the right tools and support. Thankfully, you're reading this book, showing your commitment to healing and overcoming the toxicity you've experienced.

Healing isn't a linear process and shouldn't be rushed. You'll need to take your time and do it right by implementing the nine steps discussed in this book. Use the steps discussed as a ladder that will lead you to where you need to be. For now, what's important is that you're here, learning to empower and be the best version of yourself.

You will learn to acknowledge, accept, and know narcissists' tactics before we discuss setting boundaries for them. This boundary is important to prevent them from gaining access to you and protect you from their toxicity. Then we'll focus on your healing from within and then outwardly.

At the end of this book, you will learn to prioritize self-love and boost your self-esteem and self-worth to prevent people from making you feel less of yourself.

You may wonder why I am confident that these nine steps will work. Besides being a counselor, I've lived the same experience as you. I've dated a narcissist and had to deal with the emotional baggage that comes with them. The narcissist made me feel insecure about myself and everything, that I struggled with low self-esteem. Despite having family and friends around that I could reach out to, I constantly sought approval from the narcissist, ignorant of his toxic traits. I believed that only his opinion mattered, and he represented my core worth. This false belief led me to a decade-long struggle with a toxic person.

After years of struggling to set myself free, I finally got to acknowledge and understand my emotions and behaviors. I sought help by reading many books and applying the strategies to know what works and what doesn't. I also connected with people in similar situations to learn from them. I eventually got to heal my aching heart, and I want that for many people who have been abused by toxic people.

My personal and professional experiences have helped me gain the knowledge and skills you'll see in this book. I aim to support and connect to a wider audience seeking recovery from narcissistic abuse. No matter the severity of the abuse, healing is possible, and this book serves as your guide every step of the way. Ensure you stay with me all through the steps.

This is the beginning of your healing journey, and you know yourself best. Ensure you walk your path, but keep moving forward!

Let's start this exciting journey by discussing what narcissism is and who narcissists and toxic people are.

Step One:

Clear The Air

"Nobody should be in a position where they are suffering abuse at the hands of another, and if this is the case for you, stopping the abuse by leaving the situation is the only course of action to take."

- Theresa Jackson

Welcome to a new season of your life!

When we have an issue, we commonly seek *"quick fixes"* that will only worsen the situation. To arrive at an effective solution, we'll take our time by going to the foundation of the issue and understanding how you arrived here.

Healing from narcissistic abuse can't start unless you accept that you've been emotionally abused. Clearing the air involves acknowledgment, acceptance, and knowing narcissists' tactics.

Perhaps you're unsure whether you are in a toxic relationship – this chapter aims to provide the clarity you need. It will help you see through the mask of the narcissist in your life and know them for what they truly are.

In this chapter, I explore the patterns of narcissistic relationships, signs to watch out for, and how you can recognize the narcissists in your life. As simple as these may seem, knowing them holds the key to the solution you seek.

Let's start by discussing what narcissism is and who narcissists and toxic people are.

- **What is Narcissism?**

You probably know a couple of people you believe to be narcissists. Perhaps a friend who posts one too many selfies on Instagram or a date who chattered about themselves throughout your lunch.

Narcissists are quite popular in the public imagination. We use the label "narcissist" as a buzzword for people who appear to be arrogant or "overconfident"; in short, those who we believe to be too full of themselves. In contrast, narcissism, or, more accurately, Narcissistic Personality Disorder (NPD), goes beyond overconfidence. For some reason, many believe that narcissism is rising in society, even though nothing supports this notion.

Narcissism is a spectrum. It is a trait that is distributed within the entire human population. Most people land in the middle of this spectrum, and a few find themselves at either extreme. Healthy adults who score high on the Narcissistic Personality Inventory (NPI) are those who we might consider excessively charming, even on a first encounter, but come to be recognized as shallow (Krizan & Herlache, 2017).

These healthy "narcissists" are those we perceive as arrogant or boastful. They may have awkward personal interactions from time to time but still maintain a healthy personality.

You might describe a coworker who spends too much time talking about their accomplishments as a narcissist. Still, narcissism is a tad more complicated than that. Contrary to popular belief, this trait isn't necessarily a sign of too much self-esteem or pride.

More accurately, narcissism is an excessive need for admiration, appreciation, and validation; a desire to be in the spotlight; and a hunger for special treatment due to perceived superior status. We've all met a few people whom we thought were narcissists. But true narcissists are those with Narcissistic Personality Disorder.

- **What about Narcissistic Personality Disorder?**

Narcissistic Personality Disorder (NPD) is the official term for diagnosing this mental disorder characterized by delusions of grandeur, a lack of empathy for others, and a never-ending need to be the center of attention. Individuals with this mental disorder are manipulative, self-absorbed, arrogant, and demanding. They have grandiose dreams and fantasies. They believe they are superior to others and should be given special treatment. These traits reflect in their lives, including work and relationships.

Individuals with NPD gravitate toward other people who they perceive as special or unique in some way to boost their self-esteem. They don't handle criticism and defeat quite well and seek excessive praise and admiration from others.

NPD is a diagnosable mental illness, whereas "narcissism" refers to the trait that is the hallmark of this disorder. As I said, narcissism can range in severity from person to person.

The label "narcissist" is entrenched in pop culture and sometimes overused wrongly. But as I said, narcissism exists on a spectrum. And it's healthy to have a tiny dose of this trait – it gives us the confidence to form relationships, take healthy risks, and explore life in depth. However, narcissism becomes a disorder when it interferes with day-to-day living, impairing a person's sense of self, relationships, career, and legal standing.

Anyone who has worked with or dated a narcissist will tell you that narcissists have an entirely different view of themselves than the rest of us. They treat themselves preferentially while devaluing the people around them.

Here's the rub: When you work or live with a narcissist, they expect and demand that you make everything about them. They're like a 2-year-old child that constantly needs attention. The difference is that it is appropriate for a child. You don't want a grown adult demanding that degree of attention and appreciation – and achieving it at your own expense.

A narcissist victimizes you just by being around you; they won't change – even if you ask them to. This may sound extreme if you've never found yourself in a narcissistic relationship or you're just beginning to suspect that you are in one. Listen to the story of anyone who has been the victim of a narcissistic partner. You might be shocked at just how toxic being in any relationship with these people can be.

Despite their facade of a strong personality and powerful self-esteem, narcissists don't have a core self. Their thinking, behavior, and self-image are other-centered to validate their fragile self-esteem.

- **Origin of the word "Narcissism"**

I noticed many people believe that narcissists love themselves "too much," but, in reality, narcissists don't love themselves at all. The word "narcissist" originates from the name of the Greek Narcissus. The ancient Greek gods condemned Narcissus to a life devoid of human love. Alone and lonely, he saw his reflection in a stream and fell in love. Unfortunately, Narcissus died waiting for his reflection to love him back.

Narcissists are exactly like Narcissus. They can only "love" themselves through the eyes of others. In other words, how a narcissist feels about himself is determined by how others perceive him.

The arrogant, perfect, and self-centered exterior is merely a mask for the narcissist's self-loathing. But he doesn't admit this to himself or others. Instead, he projects his true feelings about himself outward by criticizing and devaluing the people around him.

Narcissists dislike taking an authentic look inwards because they fear the truth. They are emotionally empty, so they seek to fill the emptiness with others' validation and admiration. Sadly, they are incapable of appreciating the love they get and often end up abusing and alienating those who try to love them.

There are many urban myths about narcissists. These myths are based on misconceptions formed by people without mental health credentials in an attempt to understand how narcissists begin a relationship all loving and then become cold and abusive all of a sudden.

One myth I want to explore with you is that of the narcissistic mask. The average person believes narcissists deliberately put on a "mask" to prey on unsuspecting people. This myth goes further and says that once unmasked, the narcissist runs and never looks back.

This idea about narcissists is untrue. The only ones who can pull off something so sinister are those with Machiavellianism – another trait entirely. Narcissists may have a "mask," but not in the way you think. At most, they don a mask of arrogance and overconfidence to hide their insecurities.

- **Signs That You're Dealing with a Narcissist/ Toxic Person**

You might have some ideas of what a narcissist is like, but the DSM-V specifies some traits and characteristics that must be used to determine if someone has an incredibly big ego or is narcissistic.

For an individual to be clinically diagnosed with NPD, they must exhibit at least five traits. You aren't trying to diagnose anyone with a mental disorder. Still, you should be familiar with these traits as they help identify the narcissist(s) in your life.

- An inflated sense of self-importance, exaggerating their accomplishments and gifts

- Fantasies about unlimited power, beauty, brilliance, success, and ideal love.

- Need for excessive praise and admiration.

- Lacks empathy for the feelings of others.

- Sense of entitlement

- The exploitation of others for personal ends.

- A belief that they're special and should only associate with other high-status individuals.

- Demand for special treatment from people (and institutions) and expectation of compliance with their wishes.

- Believes others are envious of them.

- Behaves arrogantly towards people.

These traits sum up someone who believes and behaves like they are above everyone else. However, you might not notice this unless you look closely at the narcissist's behavior.

Need for admiration.

A narcissist enjoys nothing more than talking about himself to a marveled audience. If you try to tell him about yourself, he will return the conversation to himself quickly. As a result, you inevitably start to feel bored, annoyed, drained, or invisible.

At the same time, many narcissists are charming, talented, good-looking, and successful. So, you may become immersed in their stunning looks and enthralling stories. Beware that the narcissist's seduction is aimed at getting your admiration and praise.

Part of the seduction is to act interested in you, but the interest declines over time. Narcissists use flattery to allure and entrap unsuspecting potential victims.

Feeling grandiose and superior to others.

Not only does a narcissist want to be the center of your world, but they also boast about their achievements and successes to impress you. You may not realize how much they exaggerated when it's a first meeting, but that's probably the case.

Even when a narcissist hasn't accomplished certain things, he may brag to you about how they intend to achieve those things or how he deserves more success than he has. The narcissist does this because he needs validation, recognition, and appreciation from you and other people.

Because he wants you to perceive him as high-status or superior, he may casually name-drop famous people and public figures he (claims to) know. Similarly, narcissists may wear expensive designers, drive luxurious cars, brag about their social circle, and invite you to the best restaurants.

The goal is to dazzle you, but it's also a sign of the constant need to present an alluring facade to prevent you from seeing into the emptiness within.

Narcissists believe their presence in your life is the key to happiness and success. This grandiose sense of self-importance makes them think they are essential to the equilibrium of others' relationships and enterprises. *"The team would have failed without me." "Who else would love you if it weren't for me?"*

Lack of empathy.

Many people who aren't narcissists lack empathy, but this trait is one of the determining symptoms of NPD, especially when paired with a sense of entitlement and exploitative behavior. Pay attention to a narcissist's expression while narrating a sad story.

They never show empathy for others' needs or hardships. I remember telling a narcissist I used to know that I wouldn't be able to make it to our date due to a family emergency. All I got was an insensitive reply: "Don't let something so trivial keep you."

Common displays of the inability to empathize with the needs of others include rudeness, walking ahead of you, not respecting your boundaries, interrupting when you're talking, not listening, ordering for you on a date without asking what you want, etc.

Admittedly, these things seem insignificant, but they indicate that this person doesn't care about you or your feelings. If they act like this with minor issues, they will behave like that on bigger issues.

Narcissists don't tolerate vulnerability, be it theirs or yours. They make it a point to keep people at arms' length because they're afraid you won't like what you see if you get too close.

Sense of entitlement.

Narcissists feel entitled because they believe they're the center of attention. Not only do they think they're unique and superior, but they also demand to be treated specially, based on this. The narcissist in your life may act like rules don't apply to him.

If he does something wrong, it's your or someone else's fault. He expects you to accommodate every one of his needs without questions – make his favorite meal whenever he wants, like his favorite TV shows, stock his favorite drinks in your refrigerator, and meet whenever he wants, no matter what you have going on.

Unfortunately, this is always one-sided. Relationships with a narcissist are never a two-way interest. The narcissist is only interested in making the relationship benefit him. You exist to meet his needs and wants, but it's never the other way around.

Exploitative behavior.

Recognizing this trait is difficult until you get close to a narcissist. However, if you're in a relationship where you feel used, that's probably because the other person is exploiting you.

For example, this person may take credit for your work. Suppose you're a woman in a relationship with a man whom you suspect to be a narcissistic partner. In that case, you may feel used as arm candy if your partner doesn't care about knowing about you beyond bragging to others about how beautiful you are.

On the other hand, a man may feel used by a narcissistic partner who is always requesting money or other things.

Narcissists use manipulation tactics to influence others to meet their needs and do their bidding. They are masters of manipulation. To many, a relationship is a game. Whether it's a romantic or familial relationship or a friendship, a narcissist doesn't care about the other person's feelings, needs, and wants. When the relationship is one-sided, the giver naturally feels exploited.

Exploitation could range from lying to cheating, gaslighting, and business or financial fraud. It may involve violations of the law.

Arrogant attitude.

Narcissists act like they're superior to you because they feel inferior. The narcissist may demean or criticize other people, ethnicities, races, or classes. Pay attention to how he treats people who provide services, such as waiters and cab drivers, compared to people of perceived high status and affluence.

A narcissist's criticism is laced with disdain and covert hostility. They don't just complain about the service; they attack the individual. How they treat people who serve them should give you an insight into how they will treat you when you fully allow them into your life.

They act like they're always right and infallible. And they never take responsibility (unless it's for something good), never apologize (unless it will serve them), and typically blame others when things don't go their way.

Based on these traits, here's how a narcissist sees himself:

- "I know you love me. Everyone loves me. No one could possibly hate me."

- "I don't need to apologize to people. They are the ones who should understand, tolerate, and accept everything I do."

- "Few people are my equals in life, and I haven't met any so far. I am the best."

- "I know there are rules and obligations, but they don't apply to me. I don't care to abide. I am not average; rules are for average people."

- "I am wonderful and without flaws. Everyone else is flawed, though."

- "No one is my equal. We are not and will never be equals. I am the smartest in the room. I achieved so and so in my career – and you should admire me for it."

- "I can criticize you, but you can never criticize me, especially in public. If you, I will never forgive or forget; I will get my pound of flesh – no matter how long it takes."

- "You should always be interested in what I have to say, but don't expect me to be concerned with your petty interests, hobbies, opinions, and achievements. I don't care."

- "I expect you to do things my way even if it is inconvenient to you. I don't care how it makes you feel – you're just weak."

- "I expect you to be grateful for anything I do, no matter how small. You, on the other hand, should simply do whatever I demand."

- "I only roll with important people and you don't measure up. You should be grateful I allow you to share my company and life."

- "If you would just act as I want, life would be much better for you."

As you can imagine, living or working with someone who thinks and behaves this way can't be easy.

From everything discussed so far, one thing should be clear: *A narcissist over values themselves and devalues others, i.e., you.* They will never treat you as an equal or respect you. At the start of your relationship, they might worship you. But, in time, they will devalue you so they can overvalue themselves.

It's good to know these traits of narcissistic people and how they view themselves compared to you, but you should also know what happens when you get involved with one. What does narcissistic love feel like? What are the patterns of narcissistic relationships? How can you recognize if you're in a relationship with a narcissistic lover? Can a narcissist really love you?

If a narcissist raised you, you're more likely to end up in a relationship with one because of the sense of familiarity. But once attached, it's difficult to exit – even when you know that the relationship is toxic and abusive. Still, it's not impossible. You can leave a toxic, narcissistic relationship if you want.

But first, you're about to discover the truth about narcissistic love.

- ## The Truth about Narcissistic Relationships

Narcissists are charming, confident, agreeable, well-adjusted, and entertaining. These traits make them easy to love. However, they are merely performances to win your love and trust. Research established that the first seven meetings with a narcissist always go so well, making it easy to fall for them. It takes much longer to see through their likable facade.

In an intimate relationship, a narcissistic partner treats you differently at home than in public. They may privately demean and devalue you after doting on you in the company of others.

Narcissistic relationships always begin with a romantic prelude, after which your partner becomes completely indifferent toward you. Once they know you're hooked, they don't see the need to continue to maintain that charming and affectionate facade.

As the excitement of a new romance wanes, the narcissist begins to show his real self. He becomes distant, dismissive, and harsh. He becomes the center of the relationship, while you are viewed merely as a vessel for validating his fragile self-esteem and ego.

In a narcissistic relationship, your abuser puts himself first and expects you to do the same. You must agree that he is the greatest lover ever and that you aren't; therefore, you should be the one who always sacrifices. Eventually, you start to feel hurt, drained, resentful, and lonely. You feel unheard and invisible, longing for the narcissist to return your love and meet your needs.

Trying to please your narcissistic lover is fruitless, like trying to fill a basket with water. He finds fault with anything you do and gives back-handed compliments when he cannot. The goal is to ensure you're always one down.

Clients, who are victims of narcissistic abuse often ask me: "Did my narcissistic partner ever love me? Why did they stop loving me?" Then, they would share a tragic story about their relationship's trajectory that I'm all too familiar with due to how many versions of the same story I have heard from other people.

He used to be so kind to me in the beginning. He told me I was perfect, that we would be together forever. He promised to always treat me well. Then everything changed so suddenly. He started ignoring me, criticizing me, finding fault with my body, and shaming me. Where did it go wrong? What did I do wrong?

Unfortunately, that is how most narcissistic relationships play out. Narcissists don't love you the way you think they do. The truth about narcissistic love is that it is idealistic and based on the narcissist's fantasy of you.

When narcissistic lovers say, "I love you," they don't mean you – they mean their idealized version of you. It always seems like they are head over heels in love with you, only because they're temporarily blinded by the idealized version of you in their mind.

Narcissistic love is shallow and superficial. It only lasts for as long as you can embody the narcissist's fantasies and meet their needs. The relationship is all about the narcissist, not you.

Sadly, victims of narcissistic abuse mistake this initial infatuation and idealization for enduring love. Narcissistic relationships don't last because they are built on fantasies. Once it's past the honeymoon stage, the narcissist starts to notice your flaws, and your fantasies are shattered. They realize you're a real person, not a Disney prince or princess.

When your narcissistic partner discovers that you're flawed like any other person, that you don't embody everything they expect or want in a lover, they begin a reconstruction project. They start to suggest "little" changes you can make to become "better."

If you reject their suggested changes, your narcissistic lover will likely become unkind and mean. As a result, arguments and fights will happen more often. And just like that, the good times start to end.

The longer the relationship lasts, the more your narcissistic lover becomes comfortable with you. Of course, they also become increasingly intolerant of your real and perceived flaws. The compliments will inevitably dry up, and here's where devaluation begins.

Suddenly, you're this ugly, stupid, and undesirable person they ordinarily wouldn't date – and the narcissist takes every chance to let you know it.

You start to hear more and more things like:

- Are you wearing *that* to the party?

- What do you think about losing a few pounds?

- How could you be so stupid?

- Don't you think you should get a personal trainer?

Naturally, you might feel compelled to make the suggested "improvements." However, they would never be enough. The narcissist would find new things to complain about. Your narcissistic lover is a perfectionist. Yet, nothing is ever as perfect as they want.

Giving in to their attempts to change you would only result in them moving the goalpost further from you. Eventually, the narcissist will abandon you – physically, emotionally, or both. Emotional abandonment is the worst in many ways. This is because the narcissist doesn't break up with you or leave you.

However, they make it clear that your wishes and well-being are now unimportant.

At this point, the narcissist may start to flirt with others in your presence or go as far as cheating. If they believe there are better options for them than you, the narcissist will eventually physically leave the relationship. You become an old toy that the narcissist no longer wants. So, they leave searching for a new toy that reality has not tainted.

The truth about narcissists is that they cannot maintain healthy, long-term relationships due to their inability to care about others. They will go the extra mile to act like a besotted lover in the early stages of a relationship, but that never lasts.

Your narcissistic spouse or lover isn't in love with the real you. They love their idealized version of you. When the fantasy falls apart (and it will), they become irritable, bored, angry, and downright nasty.

Narcissistic relationships are doomed to fall apart—try as hard as the victims of narcissistic partners try to hold them together.

Now that we've cleared the air and you know a narcissist is in your life, it's time to take the second step toward healing and recovery. Time to learn how to set boundaries in the next chapter!

Step One Takeaway

- Narcissistic abuse recovery begins with understanding who narcissists are and why they do what they do.

- Clearing the air is about acknowledgment and acceptance. Recognize the signs of abuse and accept that you're in a relationship with a narcissistic abuser.

- Healthy narcissism is not the same as Narcissistic Personality Disorder. "Narcissist" in this book refers to individuals who exhibit at least five signs of NPD, as highlighted in Step One.

- Despite the outward mask of powerful self-esteem, narcissists are incredibly insecure. They need your validation and approval to maintain a faux sense of control.

- Narcissists are incapable of truly loving others. They only pretend to "love" you for as long as you serve their needs.

- A narcissistic relationship is codependent; one person (you) gives, and the other (the narcissist) takes.

- Identifying the narcissist in your life is the first step toward recovery.

Step Two:

Set Boundaries

"Letting go of toxic people in your life is a big step in loving yourself."

- Hussein Nishah

Avoiding narcissists entirely is the best way to deal with them. However, as I stated in the previous chapter, the narcissist in your life could be a sibling, parent, coworker, boss, friend, or spouse. So, avoiding a narcissist isn't always possible unless your relationship with them becomes irreparable.

Narcissists lack empathy for the feelings and needs of others. They don't care how their actions affect you. They also feel entitled to use you as a means to an end. As a result, it can be quite challenging to establish firm boundaries with a narcissist. Still, you must do it if you want to maintain a relatively healthy relationship with the narcissist in your life.

Setting boundaries is your best bet at managing the narcissists in your life. It allows you to maintain a relationship without being affected by their self-absorbed attitude. Boundary-setting is vital to keeping your mental health, sanity, balance, and self-respect in a toxic relationship with a narcissist.

- **Why It's Important to Set Boundaries**

Interacting with individuals with pathological traits can be very challenging. Historically, psychology believed that we're in charge of our own emotions. If, for example, your parents say something unkind like, *"You will never be the first in anything! You are not good enough!"* your reaction is yours; your parents can't make you feel a certain way unless you allow yourself to feel that way. That has always been the belief.

Now, this may apply when interacting with emotionally mature people. Unfortunately, it is rarely the case when dealing with narcissistic or toxic personalities. You will experience confusion, fear, anger, guilt, outrage, and helplessness when interacting with narcissists.

What are boundaries?

Boundaries are guidelines to communicate how we want others to behave around us. Personal boundaries tell others how you want them to treat you. Therefore, they are crucial in any relationship.

The inability to set clearly defined boundaries is one of the shared qualities of victims of narcissistic abuse. That is one thing that attracts the narcissist to them in the first place.

Healthy boundary setting is a vital part of any relationship, be it romantic, familial, professional, or platonic. If you're involved with a narcissist, boundary setting is even more crucial. However, if you don't establish your boundaries firmly and effectively, the narcissist will disregard them.

One reason victims of narcissistic abuse find it hard to set boundaries is that they worry about their abuser's potential reaction. *What if he becomes meaner to me?* They might also worry about being perceived as selfish, flaky, lazy, and other things. Perhaps you also feel this way. But, as the philosopher, Lao Tzu said, "if you care what other people think, you will forever be their prisoner."

Of course, it helps to consider others' feelings when making decisions in your everyday life. That is empathy. Unfortunately, it is what narcissists lack. Still, you must not prioritize others' feelings and needs over your own. This is especially important when dealing with narcissists and toxic people generally. Otherwise, they will take advantage of you.

Many victims believe they aren't enough, so they do, do, and keep doing for others, thinking it'll eventually reach a point where they are enough for the other person. The truth is it's never enough for narcissists. If you feel like you aren't enough, it's your responsibility to address that on your own. Giving to other people won't change how you feel about yourself.

Toxic people will take until there's nothing more to take as long as you allow them. Once you set the precedent that you'll go overboard to please other people, it's hard to break that pattern. Narcissists feel entitled, so they cannot wonder if they might be asking too much of you.

Not setting firm boundaries means you'll be a bottomless well in a narcissistic relationship – just there to serve the narcissistic person's needs. The only one who can stop that cycle of abuse is you.

It's normal to feel guilt when you begin the boundary-setting process. And while that's normal, the narcissist will try to use it against you. As a result, you might think it would be better to give in to the coercion and keep yourself in the cycle of abuse, rather than endure the feeling of guilt that comes with prioritizing yourself.

Well, you shouldn't feel guilty when you get to that point. Guilt is a strong glue that keeps people in narcissistic relationships.

I believe this is due to internalized trauma. Many of us grew up modeling the relationship dynamics of parents and other adults. I know this pill may be hard to swallow, but many parents do a bad job teaching their kids to set boundaries healthily.

For example, my parents forced me to play with a kid who made me uncomfortable growing up. No matter how many times I protested, they insisted because this kid was a family friend. Some parents force their kids to do extracurricular activities they have no interest in.

Such kids may feel that they can never say no. In cases where the child finally summons the courage to say no, the narcissistic parent will make them face a world of guilt. So, the next time there's something to say "no" to, the child decides to tolerate the situation or decision instead.

It only makes sense, then, that the association of boundaries with guilt that formed in childhood will follow a lot of people into adulthood and dictate their relationships. It might even mutate into a fear of abandonment. You might fear that saying no or standing up for yourself will cause your partner to leave or your boss to fire you.

You might find it hard to learn how to establish boundaries, especially with toxic and narcissistic people, because it causes you distress. To do this, you must learn to become comfortable with this new kind of distress.

You need to be comfortable with possibly being unpopular, or maybe not being liked, or the judgments and criticism of others.

Setting boundaries in a narcissistic relationship is important because it helps you to set a tone. More importantly, enforcing established boundaries is a great way to make narcissists take responsibility for their actions and behavior, which narcissists have the hardest time doing.

Boundaries help the two parties understand what the other person expects from them. Non-toxic people respect boundaries and exhibit empathy when they violate them. On the other hand, narcissists and toxic people thrive on violating others' boundaries.

Suppose you were raised by parents who modeled respecting others' boundaries and taught you what was acceptable in interpersonal interactions. In that case, you might assume that people will naturally respect your boundaries. Sadly, this isn't always the case.

Narcissists and other pathological personalities use manipulation, gaslighting, and emotional coercion in their relationships because they weren't taught proper emotional boundary setting as children.

Further, they will disregard your thoughts, feelings, and personal space. For example, a narcissistic spouse may break promises chronically without remorse.

Continuous interactions with those who violate boundaries may make you feel violated and uncomfortable. You can recognize when your boundaries are violated in how you feel after an interaction with a narcissist.

Feeling confused, drained, exhausted, and "brain-scrambled" are all signs of boundary violation during an interaction.

Therefore, you must know how to healthily establish physical, emotional, and psychological boundaries in your relationships. That way, you feel safe, secure, and respected. The question is, how?

- **Three Parts to Setting Boundaries**

There are three parts to healthy boundary setting – identifying your boundaries, communicating your boundaries, and taking action to enforce the set boundaries. But before you can do any of these, you should know your rights in a healthy relationship. If a relationship doesn't offer you ALL of these, then it's most likely toxic and unhealthy.

What are your rights?

- To feel safe and secure.

- To define acceptable and unacceptable behavior.

- To set limits on exploitative behavior.

- To be able to say "No" and have the other person respect your boundaries and personal space.

- To feel appreciated and valued.

- To feel visible, heard, and listened to.

- To be emotionally validated.

- To have the other person meet your needs.

- To be treated with respect.

Identifying your limits – what you can and cannot accept in a relationship – is the first part of setting healthy boundaries. Ask yourself: What do I consider acceptable behavior within my relationships?

Let's say you meet someone new and exchange numbers with them. The next day, this person texts and asks you for a date, but you tell them you're busy. If they continue to text and call, you may consider them not accepting no for an answer.

An individual who doesn't take "no" for an answer is disregarding and violating your boundaries.

Boundaries vary from individual to individual. Cultural differences, personality, and social context impact it. Boundaries appropriate in a professional relationship would be irrelevant in a romantic or intimate relationship.

Identifying your boundaries is the only way to explicitly define your expectations of yourself and others in different relationships. You need self-awareness to be able to set healthy boundaries.

You must be clear about what you expect and what you are and are not comfortable with in different situations.

The second part of boundary setting is communication. It would be best to let others know the boundaries you would like them to respect. This requires you to be assertive and clear in your expectations.

Assertiveness means expressing your feelings freely and respectfully. It does not involve making demands of the other person. Rather, it entails getting people to listen to you. Healthy boundary setting cannot happen unless you learn to assert your needs and wants through self-care.

Below, I outline three key steps to communicating your boundaries to others:

1. Be clear and straightforward. State what you will and won't accept in a calm but firm voice.

2. State your needs and requests regarding what you'd like from the other person rather than what you don't like.

3. Accept any uncomfortable feeling resulting from sharing, be that shame, guilt, or remorse.

The third and final part of setting healthy boundaries is evaluating and taking action. Review your identified limits and ensure they contain everything you have in mind. Then, take the necessary steps to enforce them.

Enforcing means making sure that others learn to respect your boundaries. Boundary setting means nothing if you don't enforce established limits respectfully but firmly. Now, this is the part most people refer to when they talk about boundary setting.

Let's look at steps you can take to enforce your boundaries healthily.

- **How to Enforce Boundaries**

Next, I have seven effective approaches to enforcing your boundaries in a narcissistic relationship.

1. **Stop explaining, justifying, or defending yourself.**

A narcissist will scrutinize and intimidate you to make you second-guess yourself. Justifying, explaining, or defending yourself to them only gives the narcissist in your life power and control over you.

Part of setting boundaries is the right to choose what to share with others. Sharing your personal information with a narcissist gives them ammunition to use against you. The less you share, the less they have.

Don't feel compelled to justify your feelings or actions to a narcissist. Let's say a narcissistic coworker criticizes you; say something like, "I hear you, and I will keep what you say in mind." Suppose they criticize you, say, "I am confident in my decision." When they demand explanations, tell them it's personal or say, "We'll have to agree to disagree."

2. Decide what is tolerable and what isn't.

A key step in setting and enforcing healthy boundaries is learning to say "no" when appropriate or just for the heck of it. Think about what you're willing to tolerate from others and what you are not.

For example, you may accept mild banter but not mimicry or sarcasm. You may tolerate others passionately expressing their opinions, but reject bullying and name calling.

One way to draw the line if someone likes to call you names is to say, "I will no longer entertain conversations with you unless you start to address me with respect." Don't explain further. If the narcissist continues to behave aggressively or passive-aggressively, cease all communications with them. Do not engage them further, no matter what they say or do.

Expect the narcissist to fight back with the usual: blaming; arguing; demeaning you; acting victimized; minimizing your feelings; or gaslighting you by saying that you're too sensitive. While you will find it hard to endure these tactics, doing so communicates to them that your boundaries are not to be violated.

3. **Master the art of skillfully sidestepping critical comments and intrusive opinions or questions.**

Have you ever seen a politician skillfully maneuver difficult questions from the press by answering a different question instead – usually one they hoped would be asked? You, too, need this skill when enforcing boundaries with narcissistic people.

If a narcissistic individual asks an invasive question, swiftly change the topic. For instance, suppose you have a narcissistic parent with a track record of criticizing your career choices and relationships. In that case, don't step into the trap the next time they begin their usual interrogation. Instead, say something like, "Well, that's how we build characters, isn't it?"

Or change to something they love talking about. Ask them how they navigated difficult career choices or the secret to long-term relationships.

Their answers will be full of platitudes because that's who they are. But at least the conversation will be about them rather than you. They are their favorite topic, after all. Plus, skillfully shifting the conversation will be validating to their self-esteem.

4. **Call their actions out.**

One thing about narcissists is if they think they'll get away with doing something, they will do it. They constantly test boundaries to see what victims will let them get away with. This results from their endless hunger for attention and validation from others to counteract inner feelings of worthlessness.

You can counteract this by calling them out when they violate a boundary or do something you don't like. For example, "I notice that you stay on your phone when I'm talking to you." or "Are you trying to make me feel bad for telling you how I feel?"

State this in a matter-of-fact way. Don't worry about their reactions. Just call them out and leave it at that.

5. **Let them know the consequences of disrespecting your boundaries.**

Good boundaries come with consequences. It's not enough to state what you don't want; you must let others know what will happen if they disregard your boundaries. Consequences should be clear in your mind before a violation happens. That way, you can enforce them immediately.

When a narcissist violates your boundary, act immediately and decisively. Do this every time your boundary is ignored. Otherwise, you will lose credibility and they won't take you seriously.

Consistency is key to boundary setting. Creating boundaries is important, and remaining firm in enforcing established boundaries is just as important.

Remember the words of Eleanor Roosevelt: "No one can make you feel inferior without your consent."

- **Common Mistakes to Avoid When Setting Boundaries**

Setting and enforcing boundaries with narcissists is different from normal people because they follow different norms. There are certain mistakes you can't make with them. Once you know these and understand their reasons, coping with narcissistic individuals becomes much easier.

Avoiding the following mistakes increases your chances of establishing healthy boundaries in a narcissistic relationship.

- **Letting the narcissist in your life define you.**

A common mistake of victims of narcissistic abuse is allowing the narcissist in their life to tell them who they are. People with NPD are masters at weaving tales about who other people are and never in a favorable light.

Reject any definition a narcissist imposes on you regarding your looks, intelligence, character, career, etc. Remember that you're the only one who defines yourself. Refuse the narcissist's negative definitions; they're only projecting. Learn to define yourself positively without the narcissist's negativity.

- **Not being true to yourself.**

I know it can be hard to be true to yourself when dealing with a narcissistic partner, parent, or boss. Unfortunately, not being true to yourself is one of the biggest mistakes you can make. It implies that you've succumbed to being the giver and never the receiver.

When setting boundaries, don't think about what's best for the narcissist or the relationship you have with them. Make all decisions based on what's best for you and you alone. Up until this point, the pattern of your relationship has probably been all about what the narcissist wants, needs, demands, etc. with no regard for your wants and needs.

To change this dysfunctional pattern of relating, you must think about what's best for yourself when setting or enforcing personal boundaries. Sure, you'll get some pushback from the toxic personality and possibly fall out with them. You must expect the worst.

However, to transform into a healthier version of yourself and truly heal from narcissistic abuse, you must remain strong against any pushback.

- **Not establishing boundaries with your finances.**

Many narcissists subjugate their victims by controlling their finances. They give you spending limits or spend all the money, even when it is your money. Financial abuse is a common form of abuse. So, this isn't good for you.

It's important to separate all your finances when dealing with a narcissist. That way, the narcissist takes responsibility for their money, and you take responsibility for yours.

Assuming you're a stay-at-home mom with a narcissistic husband. In that case, I suggest you open an individual checking and savings account and start working on becoming financially independent.

Know that you have a right to participate in decision-making regarding finances even if you aren't the breadwinner.

- **Defending or justifying your actions**

Narcissists will attack you and put you on the defensive. When you notice this happening, take a deep breath and remind yourself that you don't owe them an explanation. You've done nothing wrong, so don't give in to the urge to defend yourself.

Of course, a narcissist will try as hard as possible to convince you that something is wrong with you. The goal is to make you feel bad about yourself. If you allow them to succeed, that means they've one-upped you – which they will try to do throughout the relationship.

Remind yourself of this inevitable reality and make it a point to walk away instead of engaging in the toxic dynamic.

- **Forms of Abuse to Expect After Setting Boundaries**

Narcissistic individuals consider healthy boundaries their nemesis. Establishing boundaries in an abusive relationship dynamic is like putting a formidable adversary against a toxic person. It challenges their pursuit of power and control over other people.

When you take measures to deprive them of the narcissistic supply, narcissists will respond aggressively. So, you should know what to expect when you start setting boundaries with the narcissistic parent, lover, sibling, spouse, etc., in your life.

When victims of narcissistic abuse attempt to set healthy boundaries and regain control over their lives, the abuser will completely disregard the boundaries. If they push adamantly to enforce the boundaries, the abuser will devalue, dehumanize, and invalidate them until they bow to the pressure.

You must fight to maintain your boundaries because that is the only way to win against your abuser. Plus, it will teach you to become comfortable expressing your thoughts, feelings, needs, and opinions.

This allows you to acknowledge that you are indeed being abused, forget about wanting things to be different, and break free of the narcissistic abuse cycle physically or emotionally.

Here, I describe some of the common manipulation and abuse tactics narcissists employ to violate your boundaries.

- **Gaslighting**

Gaslighting is a powerful manipulation tactic used by toxic personalities. In a narcissistic relationship, gaslighting is when your abuser invalidates your feelings so much that you begin to question whether you're right to feel that way. You might even begin to question your sanity. The worst cases of gaslighting will leave a victim unable to conceptualize their version of reality.

This is by far the worst form of narcissistic abuse because your abuser won't stop until your conception of self and reality depends on them.

Example: *"We wouldn't fight so often if you just listened to me and do what I want. You always make mistakes. You act like I'm this crazy abuser but it's just you projecting. You hurt my feelings all the time!"*

It's common for narcissists to try to gaslight victims who set firm personal boundaries. They do this to create self-doubt and self-blame so that victims can stop enforcing boundaries. Watch out for this form of abuse.

- **Hoovering**

Long-term narcissistic relationships are the worst because narcissists already know everything there is to know about their victims. From the beginning, narcissists employ the mirroring technique in a new relationship.

This manipulative tactic allows them to gather excessive information about a potential victim's identity. Then, they use the info to adapt their identity and character to fill whatever is missing in the victim's life temporarily.

With this, they are able to lay a foundation for manipulative behavior. That is how they can charm their way into potential victims' lives. Remember when you just met your narcissistic boyfriend, and he always knew exactly what you needed to hear? And later in the relationship, when he'd say just the right thing whenever you thought about leaving?

That is hoovering, and this manipulative tactic is based on the narcissist's knowledge of you. It's always reserved for when the victim enforces a strong boundary like cutting off all ties with the narcissist.

Example: *After another big fight with your abusive spouse, you pack out and temporarily move back to your parents' house. But the next day, he shows up unannounced with a large bouquet and a journal filled with thoughtful chronicles of your time together. He promised to do better and go to therapy. He told your parents he couldn't imagine a life with you, and on and on. You couldn't help giving in to his promises and gestures. Even your family was touched; they told you things would be different this time for sure.*

But they didn't, though, did they? Of course, they didn't – because that was a performance. As a victim of narcissistic abuse, you must know how narcissists hoover. They can do this independently or through other people.

Common examples include pretending to have suffered a tremendous loss. For example, they might call you to say their dog has just died. It also includes spreading lies about you or gossiping to your friends to try to manipulate them into initiating a reconciliation process.

- **Intermittent reinforcement**

Intermittent reinforcement is the irregular delivery of a reward for good behavior. If narcissists know their victim is emotionally dependent, they exploit this weakness with intermittent reinforcement. This makes it incredibly dangerous.

The narcissist gives you things that remind you of happier times. They do this to recreate the bond you felt with them in the early stages of your relationship. After a long time, the abuser becomes your only source of happiness.

So, whenever you get a "reward," it activates the reward center in your brain, flooding it with dopamine. You might not know this, but dopamine is the brain's "happy" chemical. It is the same neurotransmitter released when people use nicotine, opiates, amphetamines, cocaine, and other opioids. It can become addictive.

Narcissists commonly use intermittent reinforcement to disrupt their victims' boundary-setting process.

- **Baiting and narcissistic rage**

Baiting is one of the aggressive tactics narcissists use to distract their victim from setting firm personal boundaries. It is when they use your insecurities and vulnerabilities to lure you into an argument or confrontation.

Narcissistic rage happens when narcissists can't regulate their feelings of shame, so they mask it with displays of unbridled anger.

When you don't validate a narcissist's fragile self-esteem, it feels like an attack on their facade. This of course evokes negative emotions. A narcissist can't regulate their emotions, leading to an irrational reaction.

The narcissist either explodes into a rage or responds with the silent treatment.

- **When They won't Respect Your Boundaries**

One thing about narcissists is they need control and establishing boundaries takes that away from them. Boundaries get in the way of a narcissist's need to always be right and in control. What's the fun for them if you put a roadblock in the way?

Thus, unfortunately, the chances of a narcissist learning to respect your boundaries are slim. As a matter of fact, I don't see that happening. When you insist on enforcing boundaries, a narcissist will either leave or push back aggressively. But they will NOT give in to you.

So, if boundary setting empowers your narcissist to become even more abusive, what can you do?

The one thing you can do is leave the relationship. I know this can be hard, but you must accept that your abuser won't change. It simply won't happen. Your love isn't enough to fill the void in their soul.

Let the narcissist go and leave. Cut off all ties and don't concern yourself with what's going on in their life. Don't give them a way back into your life. Otherwise, they will hoover and find a way to restart the abuse cycle.

Healthy boundary setting is crucial to your recovery process. It is key to regaining your sanity, self-respect, and self-esteem. You need it to get back on track after escaping narcissistic abuse.

The next chapter will take you through the best ways to deal with the complex feelings that arise during your healing process.

Step Two Takeaway

- The best way to deal with narcissists is to avoid them entirely. However, you can't always eliminate the narcissist (s) in your life. In that case, the best way to deal with them is to set strong personal boundaries.

- Boundaries are a healthy way to communicate what behavior is and what isn't acceptable to the narcissist in your life. It's a key part of all interpersonal relationships.

- Not setting clear personal boundaries makes you vulnerable to narcissistic abuse.

- A narcissist most likely won't respect your boundaries, but you should firmly enforce them.

- Healthy boundary setting is a vital part of the healing and recovery process. Letting the narcissist go is the surest way to jumpstart this process.

Step Three:

Time For Healing

"You don't ever have to feel guilty about removing toxic people from your life. It's one thing if a person owns up to their behavior and makes an effort to change. But if a person disregards your feelings, ignores your boundaries, and continues to treat you in a harmful way, they need to go."

- Daniell Koepke

The aftermath of the end of a narcissistic relationship can be devastating. It isn't the same as healing from any other breakup. The things a narcissistic partner does when you try to end the relationship can leave you reeling with fear, confusion, and guilt. You must be strong and ready to navigate the end in new ways. That way, you can better protect yourself and maintain your balance.

Healing from the trauma of narcissistic abuse will be difficult, but you can pull it off. Before your healing can begin, you must first acknowledge that you were indeed abused, and it changed your life. Acknowledgment is important as it'll help you navigate the complex emotions that arise during the process.

I have made clear so far that narcissistic abuse can be subtle. It's normal to question whether you were even abused at all. But, as much as it may hurt, labeling your abuse is the first step to addressing it head-on and beginning your healing journey.

Although the process may be long and difficult, healing will refocus you on your happiness. You're not the cause of your abuse; you deserve happiness and security. What you went through doesn't define you.

Through this process, you will remember that you are strong and extraordinary. There will be good and bad times, but every day away from your abuser is another day to put a piece of yourself back. Eventually, the pieces will come together, and you will become who you're meant to be.

- **Understand That Your Feelings May Linger**

Leaving a narcissist is one of the hardest things you'll ever have to do. Unlike what many think, it isn't as simple as physically leaving, moving to a new apartment, and starting a new life.

Women, for example, typically go back to an abusive relationship seven times on average, even when they initiated the breakup. In extreme cases, a woman may lose her life during one of these seven times.

Even after permanently ending your relationship with a narcissist, you may feel connected to them. You may find it hard to stop thinking about your ex. You may randomly remember the little comments they made to make you feel like you weren't enough, how they made you feel worthless, or how you thought no one else could love you.

It may be hard to stop thinking about the good memories at the beginning of the relationship; the nice things they said; the compliments; the amazing sex; the good times you had together before everything went downhill.

This is often due to lingering feelings or trauma. As a mental health professional who works with survivors all the time, I have seen how past relationships with narcissists can continue to hold survivors back considerably – several years down the line.

Realizing that a partner has always been abusive toward you doesn't automatically make your feelings for them disappear. Feelings for an abusive ex may linger if:

- You're experiencing denial

- You're stuck in the abuse cycle

- You have an attachment style that makes you dependent on your abuser

- You observe temporary changes that inspire hope of more permanent changes

You may continue to love someone who hurt you for many reasons. Please don't take this to mean there's something wrong with you. Your feelings are valid. And thankfully, you can move past them and forge a better path for yourself.

Being a victim of narcissistic abuse can impair your self-esteem so much that you lose confidence in yourself. You will experience self-doubt. You will often feel sad and low and wonder why you even left them in the first place.

However, you should always remind yourself that leaving takes a lot of strength. And no matter how you feel in the present, you did leave, and that's the best decision you could have made for yourself. Now, you must summon all your strength and channel it into healing.

After all, the best way to give a narcissistic ex the middle finger is to become a happier and healthier you.

Healing sounds simple enough, but the process requires significant work. If you've just left the relationship, the chances of giving in to the narcissist's requests to meet so you can talk it over and they can apologize are high. That is when you're most vulnerable, and if care isn't taken, they will hook you back.

Let's be clear; the narcissist doesn't want you to have a good life. So, they will appear and disappear from your life at intervals, usually when you start to find yourself again. And sometimes, you will miss and long for them and feel the urge to reach out.

Or you might feel guilty and continue to keep in touch with them because you want to be polite. Unfortunately, that will only impede your healing as the narcissist will seize that opportunity to win you over again.

The effects of a narcissistic relationship can continue to impact your life even after cutting off all contact and entanglements.

Trauma makes the brain crave closure. And so, many survivors subsequently find themselves in similar relationships. We call this "repetition compulsion" in psychology. You may feel like someone is casting a bad magic spell on you, and with time, you feel more and more hopeless.

Even if you don't repeat the relationship and find yourself in a loving relationship several years later, you may still be haunted by the trauma of your past relationship. Decades after, you may still be looking over your shoulder, managing your PTSD with medications, work, overthinking, praying, etc.

You may wonder why humans aren't trustworthy and how someone you loved so much could hurt you that badly. Eventually, the trauma may catch up with you, and there comes a breakdown.

The trauma can even extend to the next generation. According to a 2017 systematic review of *Intergenerational Trauma in Refugee Families* published in the Journal of Immigrant and Minority Health, evidence indicates that unresolved family trauma can pass on genetically to descendants.

Suppose you leave the trauma of being in a narcissistic relationship unresolved. In that case, one or more people from your family line may end up in relationships with narcissistic abusers or become abusers.

Leaving is only the first step; the real legwork is dealing with the lingering feelings and trauma and staying gone. It's the only way to heal truly. The narcissist must leave your head, body, and soul – with no traces left behind.

Let's use this popular analogy. When there's a wound, you don't merely cover it with band-aids. No, you must clean deeply so your body can heal and rejuvenate the wound. Healing also strengthens and rebuilds the skin's surface. My point is you must tackle both roots and symptoms simultaneously when healing from narcissistic abuse.

- **Anticipate Complex Emotions**

Breakups are usually accompanied by painful feelings such as grief, a sense of loss, anger, shock, and sadness. As you undergo healing and recovery from narcissistic abuse, you will experience various complex emotions, including fear, anxiety, shame, guilt, and paranoia. I call this an emotional hangover.

The intensity and effects of these emotions can vary depending on how long you endured the relationship. The complex emotions range from mild to serious, with many survivors sustaining lifelong trauma while others recover swiftly enough.

The emotional hangover is always quite intense. It is typically characterized by profound sadness and rage. Actually, it's mostly rage masked as sadness and depression. Rage that someone you devoted yourself to who claimed to love you could treat you like that.

When the initial numbness wears off, it is replaced by intense pain and emotional distress. You will experience desperation for the pain to end, panic that you'll end up all alone, and doubt yourself for leaving. You might replay the hurt and injustice over and over in your head.

Grief is a normal thing you experience at the end of any relationship. But with narcissistic relationships, it's usually stronger. It can last weeks, months, or even years. Usually, it takes up to a year or more for the feeling to become less frequent. Even when the grief heals, it tends to leave scars.

Underlying feelings of fear and pain from being in such a restrictive, toxic relationship will eventually come to the surface. Feelings of anger and helplessness that are both depressing and out of control. You might blame yourself.

The survivors often ask me, "Where do I go from here?" "Will I ever trust again?" "How do I love again?" "Is real love even real? And will I ever find it?"

You might be tempted to withdraw, run for cover, or enter a new relationship instead of confronting the complex emotions that arise and doing the emotional work to find yourself again.

Many survivors seem to believe they shouldn't grieve the end of an abusive relationship. So, they try to suppress the feelings. But you cannot heal unless you grieve. No matter how intense the emotions are, you can endure them.

It's important to end the relationship as healthily as possible and make yourself emotionally unavailable afterward. It will make your healing significantly easier.

The effects of staying in a toxic relationship are more detrimental than the temporary pain of healing. The emotional hangover won't last forever. You will eventually experience the overwhelming relief of living without a narcissist. Imagine how you'll feel when you no longer have to walk on eggshells or explain yourself to them.

Here are some complex feelings that will arise during your recovery journey:

- **Anxiety**

Anxiety is one emotion many survivors of narcissistic abuse live with. After leaving the narcissist, you may experience extreme anxiety as you navigate new friendships and relationships. Individuals who leave abusive relationships often get separation anxiety, resulting in panic and disorientation when they aren't with their abusers. You might get anxiety attacks or become hypervigilant.

The good thing is these symptoms will decrease over time, especially if you work to overcome your trauma instead of letting it define you.

- **Depression**

Many individuals who leave narcissistic relationships also struggle with depression. After years of listening to how worthless and unlovable they are, they may experience feelings of worthlessness. It's common for victims to go into isolation, which only worsens the depression.

- **Post-Traumatic Stress**

As a survivor of long-term narcissistic abuse, you will experience symptoms of post-traumatic stress. The trauma of an abusive relationship rewires the brain's fear center, keeping you in a perpetual "fight or flight" state. As a result, your brain will remain on alert, always looking out for a threat. Anything associated with the traumatic memories can trigger a panic attack.

You become hypervigilant, feeling the need to always be on guard. Many victims mention not knowing what their abusers would do next. Chronic hypervigilance can make healing even harder because it keeps you on the lookout.

As a result, you may avoid certain situations and things that trigger memories of your abuse. This could be as severe as steering clear of places you used to hang out with the narcissist or mutual friends and acquaintances.

- **Loss of sense of self**

It's common for narcissistic abuse survivors to feel like they don't know who they are. Narcissists use gaslighting and other techniques to brainwash their victims. These tactics can destroy a person's sense of self, inducing feelings of worthlessness. You may not remember who you were before the unfortunate relationship began.

Many survivors even struggle to recognize themselves in the mirror. They can no longer see their reflection.

You may develop trust issues in other relationships, especially intimate ones. You may find that you now second-guess yourself when making decisions. Feeling like you played a part in the abuse can evoke shame and guilt, holding you back from seeking professional help.

- **Emotional lability**

After experiencing something as traumatic as narcissistic abuse, you may suffer erratic mood swings and irritability. In some cases, you may feel emotionally dead, like a robot. You might feel detached from reality and everything around you. This is called depersonalization, which many abuse victims report experiencing.

Complex emotions aside, survivors of narcissistic abuse also suffer certain physical symptoms. Trauma usually stores itself in the body and manifests as headaches, body aches, stomach aches, and other physical illnesses.

You may develop sleeping problems. Post-traumatic stress can make it hard to shut off your brain at bedtime. And when you sleep, you could have nightmares that haunt you during the daytime.

It's common for victims also to suffer cognitive problems, such as the inability to focus and short-term memory loss.

- **Steps to Healing from Abuse**

The mind and heart often have two different views regarding healing from abuse. But the key to healing lies in letting your heart and mind communicate.

The heart says: *I love him/her.*

The mind says: *You must get over them. They abused you. Go far away and never look back.*

You should listen to the mind. However, that isn't always easy. If it were, everyone would heal from abuse so quickly. The back-and-forth between your mind and heart will go on for as long as you let it, leaving your trauma unresolved.

They have two entirely different perspectives on the same situation. The heart focuses on how good you felt when things were rosy, while the mind focuses on how everything turned sour. It would be best if you didn't passively wait for something to happen to break the dialogue. You can make things happen on your own.

You can take steps to speed up healing and recovery and, more importantly, end the destructive internal dialogue tearing you apart.

First, you must cease all contact and block all communication paths. In some situations, such as co-parenting, you can't simply erase this abuser from your life. However, you can create modified contact and adhere strictly to it. This means setting up all communications regarding your kids via third-party channels. And if you need to make agreements, ensure you set up court orders.

Next, you need to release the trauma from your mind and body. This means doing the opposite of our natural urge – which might be to try and fix the narcissist. Believing that you can help a narcissist is the result of codependency. You must turn this thinking pattern around and look internally. Forget about the narcissist and focus on yourself.

Once you stop looking to fix the narcissist and start looking to heal inside instead, your trauma will start releasing, and relief and balance will rise in you again.

Forgiveness is a key part of your healing journey. If you don't forgive the wounded and damaged parts of yourself, you may be unable to stop seeking companionship from toxic people. I know that it can be hard to forgive yourself, especially if the narcissist hurts other people in your life.

You may also believe that you can't possibly rebuild your life from everything you lost to the abuser. This is particularly true for people who escape from abuse in middle age.

Forgiving yourself is the only way you can find acceptance and resolution. You can learn to reject old patterns of not loving or respecting yourself. Know that the experience was only a part of your learning in life.

Release the self-judgment and regret. Once you do this, reclaiming your life becomes simple. You will become hopeful once again.

Next, I have an exercise that would help fast-track your healing process.

Exercise: Challenge your dysfunctional beliefs

Begin this exercise by writing down your beliefs about your narcissistic relationship. These should be beliefs that are impeding your healing process.

For example:

- *I could have made it work with him.*

- *It was partly my fault that he treated me so unkindly.*

- *He has a new girlfriend, and he's treating her better than he ever treated me. That is proof that this new person is better than me.*

- *I will never find someone to love me again.*

These beliefs come from the emotional side of your brain. Your heart longs for what you once had with the narcissist when the relationship was at its peak. You're struggling to confront the pain of accepting your new reality – that the relationship you hoped would last forever just crashed because your partner isn't who you thought they were.

You know there's nothing to salvage except lessons, yet you cannot face this realization head-on. Instead, you try to convince yourself that you can still make the relationship work if you give the narcissist another chance.

The second step in this exercise is to think about your childhood: Did someone from then encourage you always to take the blame?

Most survivors I have met blamed themselves for ending a toxic relationship because they had a parent who blamed them disproportionately. If you can relate to this, it would help to see that you can't assess your current situation realistically because your childhood is replaying itself.

Example – *You had a narcissistic mother who blamed you anytime something went wrong. When she yelled at you, she blamed you for making her lose her temper. And when the milk went sour, it was your fault for leaving it out.*

Next, think about why you blame yourself. Why do you protect your abuser and blame yourself instead? We don't always blame ourselves because of past trauma. We do it to serve a psychological purpose. To move on, you must recognize what psychological purpose you're serving by blaming yourself. Perhaps you think blaming yourself means you can work on making it better. Or accepting that they abuse you means letting them go completely, and you're afraid of that. Think about this deeply.

Now, this is the final part of this exercise. Remember the dysfunctional beliefs you wrote down at the beginning of this exercise? Go back to them and write down a true statement that contradicts them. Ensure you write only what your mind tells you.

Example:

False Belief	True Statement
I could have made it work with him.	*There's nothing I could have done to change the outcome. He was the problem, not me.*
It was partly my fault that he treated me so unkindly.	*I don't agree that it is my fault. I am not the only person he treated like this.*
He has a new girlfriend, and he's treating her better than he ever treated me. That is proof that this new person is better than me.	*Treating women well, in the beginning, is his modus operandi.*
I will never find someone to love me again.	*I will find a new man who will love me and treat me exactly how I want.*

Whenever you catch yourself longing for your abuser or blaming yourself, read out the true statements aloud.

- **Exercises to Heal Your Mind**

The trauma of suffering narcissistic abuse changes you forever. While many believe that trauma-based changes are always negative, that isn't true. Traumatic experiences heighten your senses, leaving you overwhelmed and out of control. If not resolved, you can get stuck in that heightened state for the rest of your life.

We often refer to trauma as the body's response to abnormal events. When you're living a traumatic experience, your body responds with tense muscles, pain, lack of focus, and insomnia. These trigger intense emotional experiences of anxiety, fear, confusion, paranoia, and other emotions. So, trauma affects the body and mind.

Connecting your physical and emotional responses can be challenging, but it is key to healing. Exercise can help you make this crucial connection.

Exercise is an effective way to open communication between your mind and body. You must understand that the effects of trauma store themselves in the body. No matter the cause of trauma, whether physical or psychological, your body will retain symptoms of your traumatic experience.

It's been well-reported that physical exercise has many benefits for the body and mind. Regular exercise positively affects every part of the body.

Somatic therapy is a well-known approach to resolving trauma. It teaches you to tune into your physical sensations to release traumatic energy. You will find somatic therapy particularly helpful if you have post-traumatic stress resulting from narcissistic abuse. '

Here, I have some exercises based on this approach that you can practice at home. These exercises are body-focused and can help if your body is stuck in a state of heightened sensations, i.e., the stress response.

These exercises will help you regain your body/mind connection. This will make it easier to regulate complex emotions that arise during your healing process. A 2017 study on *Somatic Experiencing for Posttraumatic Stress Disorder* by Danny Brom et al. found that somatic therapy relieved symptoms of depression and PTSD.

So, what are some exercises you can try?

Grounding

Grounding techniques help you to center yourself in the present moment. This takes your mind off past events, thus reducing your distress. You will find grounding exercises particularly helpful if you have anxiety or flashbacks. It also helps with depersonalization.

Some grounding techniques you can try include:

- **Run cold water over your hands.** Notice how the water feels from your wrist to the nails when you do this. Pay attention to the temperature. Then, run some warm water and notice the change in sensation. Do this for a few minutes. It will help you calm down.

- **Focus on your breath.** Inhale to the count of 4, hold your breath to 3, and exhale to another count of 4. Focus on the rise and fall of your belly as you inhale and exhale. Notice the feel of air when you breathe out.

Body Scans

This is an active meditation exercise to help you relieve anxiety and other physical symptoms of post-traumatic stress. Here's how to do a body scan:

- Sit comfortably in a chair with your feet firm on the ground and close your eyes. Make sure to take off your shoes.

- Start with your feelings. Notice how it feels on the floor. Then, move upward to your ankles, knees, and thighs. Notice the tension, pressure, and other physical sensations as you scan upward.

- Now, do the same with your upper body. Scan from your waist to your stomach, chest, neck, head, and face.

Apart from these somatic therapy-based exercises, you should also engage in physical activities to heal your mind from trauma. You might not like working out, and that's fine.

Taking long walks, moving to yoga videos, riding a bike, and roller skating also help. You can even have regular solo dance parties to your favorite tunes. Any activity that involves physical movement will contribute significantly to your healing, so do whatever works.

If you like working out, I have some exercises that will help you greatly. A rule of thumb is to begin slowly with low-intensity exercises and gradually work up to full capacity.

Aerobic exercises are especially good for restoring emotional and physical health. They can help relieve stress, build resilience, and increase the production of depleted hormones such as dopamine, serotonin, and endorphins.

Various aerobic exercises such as brisk walking, jogging, and swimming can increase BDNF (brain-derived neurotrophic factor) – a chemical that stimulates brain cell creation. It also increases activity in the hippocampus, the part of your brain responsible for managing trauma-based stress.

Opt for low-impact activities unless you're used to engaging in high-impact activities regularly.

Flexibility exercises, strength training, and balance training are also incredibly important for various reasons. You can start with 2-3 sessions a week and slowly work up to five sessions weekly.

The more you engage in physical activities, the faster you can release trauma from your body and mind.

Exercise gives you a feeling of increased control over yourself, including the parts of you that trauma has made difficult to recognize. It is a powerful engine of the healing process.

The next step is about breaking the vicious cycle of narcissistic abuse. I will take you through the steps to break free from narcissistic abuse. More importantly, we will discuss how you can ensure you don't pass on the trauma to your kids and future generations.

Step Three Takeaway

- Healing from a narcissistic relationship isn't the same as healing from the end of a normal relationship.
- The narcissist will fight back aggressively when you try to leave them; that's if they don't leave you first.

- As you navigate your healing process, you will experience complex negative emotions and physical symptoms.

- Self-forgiveness and self-compassion are important throughout this process because they reinforce your emotional health.

- Healing takes time; therefore, it won't happen overnight. Put in the work, and you'll see the gain. Healing will refocus you on your happiness.

Step Four:

Break the Vicious Cycle of Narcissistic Abuse

"A narcissist paints a picture of themselves as being the victim or innocent in all aspects. They will be offended by the truth. But what is done in the dark will come to light. Time has a way of showing people's true colors."

- Karla Grimes

As you may already know, the narcissistic abuse cycle is a vicious and damaging pattern of behavior that is all too common in relationships where one partner is a narcissist. This cycle can be difficult to break free from, but you can do it with the right help and support. It's important to recognize the signs of the narcissistic abuse cycle so that you can understand what is happening in your relationship and take steps to protect yourself.

- **Understanding the Narcissistic Abuse Cycle**

Lenore Walker conceptualized the theory of the *cycle of abuse* in 1979 to contextualize abuse against women in intimate relationships. This theory identifies a pattern of repeated events that occur in abusive relationships.

Four stages characterize the abuse cycle: Tension, Incident, Reconciliation, and Calm. In the past, people believed that a relationship had to be physically violent to be considered toxic or abusive. Walker's theory of the cycle of abuse contributed to changing this perception of abuse in romantic relationships.

A narcissistic relationship is typically marked by emotional and psychological abuse, which is just as damaging as physical abuse. Intimate Partner Violence (IPV) is linked to narcissistic relationships in the context of psychological and emotional, and physical abuse.

In addition, psychology researchers have established that covert narcissists, especially female narcissists, tend to use the cycle of abuse to maintain control in their relationships.

Individuals with strong narcissistic leanings and those with NPD are manipulative and highly controlling. Remember that many people have strong narcissistic traits without being clinically diagnosed with Narcissistic Personality Disorder.

Healthy relationships demand transparency, honesty, and genuine expression of emotions. However, narcissistic individuals are unable to tick these boxes. They might pretend in the early phase of a new relationship, but they eventually get tired of the charade.

And that's when the mask comes off. The exhaustion of posing as a healthy, equal partner precedes the narcissistic abuse cycle.

The narcissistic cycle of abuse is a pattern where a highly narcissistic individual utilizes manipulative behaviors and tactics to devalue their partners. This cycle differs from the four-stage abuse cycle conceptualized by Lenore Walker.

I have made abundantly clear so far that a relationship with a narcissistic partner is typically one-sided. In most cases, the relationship exists to meet the needs of the narcissistic partner. The narcissist enforces this through the cycle of abuse.

Lenore's original cycle of abuse can be adapted to narcissistic relationships. Just as we now know physical violence in a relationship isn't gender-specific, many are starting to learn that narcissistic abuse is unisex.

Instead of physically hurting someone, many narcissistic individuals use gossip and lies to besmear their victim's social standing. They may use any means necessary to control the narrative in the partnership and ensure the other person remains in line. Even when called out, the narcissist may declare that the victim deserves everything they get.

Before we delve into the stages of the narcissistic abuse cycle, I want to note that the cycle is a continuous pattern. Therefore, there is no "first" or "last" stage. It just keeps happening without a clear beginning or end.

Additionally, we're focusing on how narcissistic people use the cycle of abuse to manipulate their victims into meeting their demands. It's all about forcing the victims to ebb and flow according to their abuser's whims.

So, what are the three stages of the narcissistic cycle of abuse?

1. Idealization

This is the first stage of narcissistic abuse. I consider this the most dangerous stage because it is how the narcissist hooks you. It always happens in the beginning phase of a relationship with a narcissist.

Idealization is where the narcissist love-bombs you and presents a false image of your ideal partner. They overwhelm you with love, affection, adoration, and gifts to hook you. They get you the right thing at the right moment, so much so it feels like they have a sixth sense that tells them what you want or need.

During the idealization phase, you may find just being around the narcissist intoxicating. You feel like you can't get enough of them. You synchronize so easily that you wonder how lucky you are to have found someone that perfectly aligns with you. This is where the narcissist convinces you there is a perfect synergy between you that could last forever.

The narcissist may take you on dates to the best restaurants; take you on adventures and vacations; shower you with amazing gifts; and share cutesy notes confessing their love to you every day. Don't get me started on the compliments – you will feel so good that you'll mistake these red flags for green ones.

Within a short period, you may think this might be "the one" for you. In turn, you relax your boundaries to accommodate them. After all, this is your perfect mate – why shouldn't you let your guard down?

Even when the narcissist starts to showcase a few "red flags," you quickly find excuses and justifications for their behavior. *"He only yelled at me because he had a bad day. He wouldn't do that ordinarily. Justin is not that kind of man." "She told me all about how her past relationship hurt her. I need to be more lenient."* You might even blame yourself for the narcissist's behavior.

Usually, when the spell vaporizes, many victims think the narcissist is playing games at this stage. But this isn't always true. For many narcissists, they mean everything they say at this stage.

As I explained in the previous chapter, it isn't truly you the narcissist is in love with. Rather, they are in love with an idealized version of you in their mind. You're merely a character in the "love script" the narcissist has written, and it's all projections.

This stage typically includes the following behavior:

- Love bombing
- Grand gestures
- Elaborate dates and gifts
- Lots of attention – almost overwhelming

- Minor boundary violations

- Isolating the victim in the name of love

- Fast-paced intimacy

The idealization stage is the honeymoon phase of a narcissistic relationship. Once this phase is over, the second stage – devaluation – subtly begins, and the narcissist gradually lifts the facade you've become accustomed to in the idealization stage.

2. Devaluation

Usually, when the honeymoon phase wears off, normal couples follow a routine they create together. Most couples become more intimate and adapt problem-solving skills as their relationship grows. Unfortunately, this is far from what happens in a narcissistic relationship.

Once the narcissist knows you're fully drawn in, they switch up and start devaluing you. They suddenly push you off the pedestal they place you on. This is where they start to notice your flaws and realize that you aren't as perfect as the idealistic character in their love script.

The narcissist will manipulate you. They will start subtly, focusing on seemingly trivial things at first. They may isolate you from your loved ones, including your closest friends and family. They do this to make you completely dependent on them.

By isolating you from your loved ones, the narcissist neutralizes your support network, making it hard to share your sufferings with others. This means you become your only support network. It's a classic divide-and-conquer tactic.

Over time, the narcissistic individual will become verbally (and sometimes physically) abusive. They will insult, demean, shame, blame, accuse, and guilt-trip you. They will lie, deceive, and distort facts to gaslight you. They will deliberately withhold love, affection, physical intimacy, money, and other needs while simultaneously imposing on you to meet their needs and demands.

The narcissistic partner may use mockery and sarcasm to shame you publicly. They do this to attack your self-esteem and put you in your place. More importantly, they do it to maintain their illusion of power and control over you. The narcissist often becomes aggressive and uses narcissistic rage to enforce submission. In the worst cases, they become physically violent.

During the devaluation stage, it is common for victims to justify and excuse the narcissist's behavior. This is partly due to the attachment developed in the first stage. In classic narcissistic style, abusers occasionally switch up the abuse cycle with a little love-bombing whenever necessary. They do this to confuse and engage you. And it tends to work. When you confront them, the narcissist will act like the victim.

Devaluation often makes victims start to doubt themselves. You may feel like everything is your fault and you aren't good enough. This phase slowly chips away at your self-esteem until you don't even recognize who you are anymore.

The devaluation phase typically includes the following behaviors:

- Attempting to change you

- Increasing insults and criticism

- Gaslighting

- Lack of communication

- Triangulation

- Increased isolation

- Withholding of emotional, physical, and sexual intimacy

- Increased boundary violations
- Increased isolation from friends and family
- Physical threats

Next is the third phase of the narcissistic cycle of abuse.

3. Rejection

In healthy relationships, couples navigate conflict with calm and grace. Both partners work together to solve issues and resolve conflicts. But that's not how narcissistic relationships are. In the rejection stage, narcissists blame their partners for all disagreements and conflicts. Once they no longer want to deal with this reality of all relationships, the narcissist discards their partner.

They no longer want love or security. You can no longer fill the void in their soul with your affirmations and validations, so they reject you.

The thing about toxic relationships is that the narcissistic partner is always in it for a selfish purpose. At the early stage, this may have been money (if you're wealthy), beauty, the prestige of being in a relationship with you, and in many cases, the thrill of the "chase."

Once they've served their selfish purpose, and you no longer offer anything new, the narcissist sees no reason to stay in the relationship. Or if you've undermined their facade in any way, they will pull the rug from under you. Then, the narcissist will move on and look for a "better" model to feed their ego.

Suppose you exit the relationship before they can. In that case, you will most likely incite the narcissist's wrath. To them, you become an enemy that must be destroyed at all costs. It's a double-edged sword.

If the narcissist doesn't move on and you don't end the relationship, the cycle of abuse will continue until something happens and you finally leave them.

The rejection phase typically includes the following behavior:

- Invalidating your feelings
- Blaming you for the impending downfall of the relationship
- Playing the victim
- Emotional and physical abuse
- Contempt and rage
- Feelings of a deep betrayal

- Ending the relationship

- Hoovering

Narcissists perpetuate the cycle of abuse to devalue and demoralize their victims further. So, how does this cycle typically play out in a narcissistic relationship?

- **Defining Event.** A crisis happens, prompting an outburst from the narcissist. This could be a fight, an argument, or a miscommunication. It may be real or imagined. No matter the cause of the drama – even a minor inconvenience – the narcissist uses it as an excuse to explode. They might do this because of a sense of losing control over you. The goal is to use the event to refocus attention on themselves.

- **Power shift.** Even if the narcissist is responsible for the crisis, you're the one who ends up apologizing. The outburst, i.e., defining event shifts power back to the narcissist, and you get all the blame. You end up apologizing to keep the peace or because you feel helpless. Learned helplessness is a key reason behind the repetition of the phases of the narcissistic abuse cycle.

- **Peace and quiet.** There is a cool-down period where everything feels quiet and peaceful. But this is only on the outside. Internally, you're constantly thinking of ways to "make it up" to your abuser – even though you've done nothing wrong. The narcissist sees this and further manipulates the situation to make themselves the victim and you the aggressor.

- **Tension buildup.** Over time, the narcissist starts to lose control again. Things have been quiet and normal, but neither of you is comfortable with the quiet. Out of fear, tension starts to build up. You're afraid of the narcissist, while the narcissist is afraid of losing control over you and the relationship. It's only a matter of time before another outburst and display of narcissistic rage; then, the cycle repeats itself.

All relationships have cycles of peace and conflict. Sadly, conflict is inevitable in healthy relationships. There will be times when you or your partner will go through interpersonal crises or face major life challenges.

However, the difference between a standard relationship cycle and the narcissistic cycle of abuse is the power imbalance.

- **The Impact of the Narcissistic Abuse Cycle**

Narcissistic abuse impairs your sense of self, your sense of reality, and your sense of emotional security. It makes you feel like you're too sensitive. Victims tend to feel like they're blowing things out of proportion when narcissists behave unacceptably. This especially happens when the abuse cycle is devoid of physical abuse and violence.

If narcissistic abuse continues for too long, it often results in a victim developing mental health conditions, such as anxiety, depression, post-traumatic stress, and dissociation. A 2019 study titled *Recognizing narcissistic abuse and the implications for mental health nursing practice* found that narcissistic abuse is sometimes fatal. So, that's how serious the impact of the narcissistic abuse cycle can be.

With that in mind, here are five things that depict the impact of the narcissistic cycle of abuse.

1. **You feel isolated.**

Narcissistic abuse isn't always obvious to third parties. If you try to communicate the true state of your relationship to loved ones, they might not understand since your spouse is the perfect lover on the outside.

This can make you feel alone and more vulnerable to narcissistic manipulation. The narcissist may draw you back with apologies and kindness or pretend the abuse doesn't exist.

If you're in a relationship where you feel alone and without a support network, that is most likely an abusive relationship.

2. You freeze up.

Victims of narcissistic abuse have different responses to trauma. Some try to confront their abuser (fight), whereas others try to flee the situation (flight). If neither method works or you feel helpless, you might respond with "freeze."

"Freeze" is a stress response triggered when a person feels utterly helpless. It often involves dissociating from the situation. Creating an emotional distance between you and your abuser can help decrease the intensity of the abuse. This numbs your pain and distress.

Freezing sometimes helps, but it's not the best response in a narcissistic relationship since you *can* flee the situation. Yet, you might stay if you think there's no way out. You might even switch to fawning, which means doing everything to keep your abuser happy.

3. **You find it hard to make decisions.**

Devaluation can leave your self-esteem and confidence completely wrecked. Over time, you start to absorb your abuser's insults and criticism, and they start to inform your self-perception. This can make you lose confidence in your decision-making skills.

The uncertainty that comes with experiencing the narcissistic abuse cycle can impair your ability to make even the simplest decisions.

4. **You get unexplained physiological and physical symptoms.**

Abuse triggers anxiety, which often leads to physical symptoms. These include appetite changes, nausea, upset stomach, stomach ache, muscle aches, insomnia, gastrointestinal distress, and fatigue. You might start using alcohol, drugs, and other substances to manage these symptoms, especially fatigue and insomnia.

5. **You feel restless and nervous.**

Narcissistic abuse, like all forms of abuse, is usually unpredictable. You may not know whether to expect criticism or a grand gift. Since you never know what to expect from the narcissist at any given time, you might develop restlessness and tension from always preparing yourself for conflict.

You lose the ability to relax since letting your guard down around the narcissist makes you feel unsafe.

- **How to Break Free**

Breaking free from the narcissistic cycle of abuse can seem impossible. You will be exhausted through devaluation, gaslighting, and the never-ending conflict. So, you might feel too tired to make a move. But you can break free if you set firm boundaries and never stop reminding yourself why it's best to walk away from the toxic relationship.

Here are some tips to help you get out of the toxic situation and finally leave that narcissist in your life behind forever.

- **Don't give any more chances.** The average victim needs up to seven tries to leave an abusive relationship completely. If the narcissist isn't ready to let you go, they will use every means possible to ensure you stay. But no matter what, do not give in to the cry for "one more chance." You can risk it.

- **Understand that the narcissist will never change.** One of the biggest mistakes you can make is thinking the narcissist will change. Don't try to change them because it's practically impossible. Unless the narcissist agrees and commits to intensive therapy, they will not change.

- **Don't let them know you're leaving.** If you do, they will do everything possible to stop you. The narcissist will intensify their love-bombing efforts to keep you emotionally connected, or they will become more abusive. Both tactics can negatively impact your physical and mental wellness and safety.

- **Assemble a support team.** Leaving will take a toll on you emotionally and psychologically. You will need an emotional support network to help you start and go through with it. Your team may include a divorce attorney, therapist, friends, and family members.

- **Do not argue with the narcissist.** Avoid arguments at all costs – it only makes them feel more powerful. Do not engage with them. One statement is all the narcissist needs to explode into narcissistic rage.

- **Have your own money.** If you want to leave a narcissistic partner, you must have your own money and bank account. Do this in advance to reduce your financial dependency on your abuser. If your partner is a financial abuser, do this secretly. Otherwise, they might cut you off completely if they find out about your plans to leave.

- **Stay away from the narcissist completely.** Keeping in touch is dangerous because your abuser can seduce you to come back. The brain is adept at reminding us of all the good times after a bad breakup. Don't fall victim to this. When you leave, ensure you stay left.

The narcissistic cycle of abuse can traumatize and emotionally scar you. Familiarize yourself with the phases of abuse to become better at recognizing the pattern and remove yourself from a potentially toxic situation as soon as possible.

The best way to start dealing with the impact of narcissistic abuse is to pump up your self-esteem and sense of self-worth. So, that's what we'll be discussing in the next step. The fifth step of recovering from narcissistic abuse is all about helping you turn up the dial on your self-esteem again.

Step Four Takeaway

- This cycle can be difficult to break free from, but you can do it with the right help and support.

- The narcissistic cycle of abuse is a pattern where a highly narcissistic individual utilizes manipulative behaviors and tactics to devalue their partners. This cycle differs from the four-stage abuse cycle conceptualized by Lenore Walker.

- The three stages of the narcissistic cycle of abuse are Idealization, Devaluation, and Rejection

- If narcissistic abuse continues for too long, it often results in a victim developing mental health conditions, such as anxiety, depression, post-traumatic stress, and dissociation.

- You can break free if you set firm boundaries and never stop reminding yourself why it's best to walk away from the toxic relationship.

Step Five:

Pump Up Your Self-Esteem & Self-Worth

"Narcissists burn your sanity, erode your self-esteem, and make you doubt your own judgments and perceptions."

- Invajy

Self-esteem and self-worth are often used interchangeably because both concepts deal with how people perceive or feel about themselves. The goal is to have strong self-esteem - you feel good about yourself most of the time.

Humans should understand that we're intrinsically valuable. And we're good and worthy people, even when we make mistakes. Having strong self-esteem doesn't mean thinking you're better than others.

Individuals with high self-esteem know and accept their strengths and weaknesses. They recognize their good qualities and areas where they need to improve. They are confident and capable, yet they know they are imperfect.

Sadly, many individuals don't feel good about themselves. They don't feel confident, capable, or worthwhile. They also fixate on their flaws and imperfections. These people have usually experienced trauma – abandonment, rejection, infidelity, betrayal, and abuse. People in relationships with highly narcissistic individuals fall into this category.

You may have had low self-esteem when you met the narcissist, but a narcissistic relationship can deplete your self-esteem further. Even if you didn't, your self-esteem and sense of self-worth have likely been negatively impacted throughout your relationship with a highly narcissistic partner.

You must start rebuilding your self-esteem and self-worth because it's the key to avoiding toxic and narcissistic partners in the future.

- **How Narcissistic Abuse Affects Self-Esteem and Self-Worth**

If you grew up with a parent or guardian with NPD or strong narcissistic traits, your sense of self was probably damaged during your upbringing. Your sense of self impacts nearly every aspect of your life. Unfortunately, you may not know how having a poor sense of self affects your life. It's impossible to miss something you never knew you had.

An individual's sense of self is "this is who I am" or "this is who I am not." Suppose you were raised by a narcissistic parent who violated your boundaries early on. In that case, you were raised by a controlling parent in a highly regulated environment. Your parents might have told you that your opinions and ideals are useless. That can make it extremely hard to clearly define who you are, who you aren't, what you like, and what you don't like.

Narcissistic abuse in childhood lays the foundation for getting into narcissistic relationships as an adult. Believe me; narcissists can sniff out trauma from miles away. That is why they seek relationships with codependent people who narcissistic parents most likely raised.

The experience of narcissistic abuse can make you become so externally focused on the people around you, initially, your narcissistic parent and then other people you meet later in life. As a result, you may have a poor sense of who you are.

How would you reply if someone asked you who you are right now? Perhaps you'd reply that you're a son, a daughter, a mother, a sister, a father, a brother…but, other than that, who are you?

One of the effects of narcissistic abuse is that your likes, dislikes, wants, needs, desires, and values become synchronized to the likes, dislikes, needs, wants, desires, and values of the narcissist and other people in your life. It becomes impossible to define who you are and your needs and desires. If your narcissistic abuse experience began in childhood, you likely don't value yourself. People with low self-esteem tend to define their value by what they can do for others instead of what they need for themselves.

Being in a relationship with someone who always says you're the problem or you're stupid, weak, and incapable can make it hard to trust your judgments and perceptions. This is one of the ways narcissistic abuse affects self-esteem and self-worth.

Additionally, the volatile nature of a narcissistic relationship can make you feel the need to walk on eggshells. You learn to minimize your needs and feelings to keep the narcissist happy. You discount your wants and needs and believe you're wrong to have them. You stop asserting yourself and become passive. All of these are signs of how narcissistic abuse is affecting your self-esteem.

Narcissistic abuse affects your self-esteem and self-worth by making you feel:

- There's something wrong with you.

- Useless – you have no value and you aren't good enough.

- Disconnected from your core self.

- Self-critical.

- Afraid to assert yourself, turning you into a people-pleaser and pushover.

- Like you can't trust yourself or make decisions for yourself.

Rebuilding your self-esteem after leaving a narcissistic relationship can be hard. Building your self-esteem is next to impossible if you're still in an abusive relationship. So, I encourage you to leave as quickly as possible and seek help from your support network.

Pumping up your self-esteem and self-worth begins by reminding yourself that you aren't what your narcissistic ex and others say about you.

- **You're Not The Many Things That Your Ex (Or Others) Say About You**

When you leave an abusive relationship where your partners used to berate and criticize you harshly, it's normal to struggle with moving on. The hurtful words and harsh judgments can have a lasting impact on your self-esteem if you allow them.

Your ex's harsh words will have an even more damaging impact if you internalize them instead of letting them go. It's important to release the hurt and pain from the past relationship. Understand that those words don't define who you are and don't reflect your true value.

It's in a narcissist's nature to tear their victim down with hurtful words, especially when they know you're walking away. They will tell you many things: "*You won't survive without me*", "*Nobody else can love you because you're unlovable. I'm the only one who can put up with you!*"

These may sting, but the aim is to make you feel like they are your best and only chance. But you must realize that leaving the toxic relationship is what will set you on the path to the best years of your life. Let the narcissist go with the belief that you're destined for better things.

You must not define your value by what others say about you. When you label yourself with the words your abuser used, shut it down immediately and remind yourself that you're valuable to yourself and your loved ones.

For every negative comment you remember, counter it with a positive affirmation. *I am strong. I am capable. I am worthy of love. I am good enough.*

Build a positivity fortress so you can rise above your past and start rebuilding your self-esteem.

- **End Negative Thoughts**

Everyone engages in negative thinking when life gets challenging and overwhelming. But individuals suffering from narcissistic abuse experience a nonstop stream of negative thoughts daily without realizing it.

Negative thinking becomes so ingrained that you don't even know when you're engaging in this destructive behavior. Since you've become accustomed to thinking negatively about yourself due to the usual barrage of criticism and insults from the narcissist, it's easy to conclude that negative thoughts are benign.

But negative thoughts lead to negative emotions, which make you feel bad about yourself. This creates a negativity loop that destroys your sense of self every day. The more you engage in negative thinking, the lower your self-esteem becomes. This makes it hard to make decisions or take actions that will lead to the life you truly desire.

The negativity loop operates in a way that negative thoughts create an ideal environment for low self-esteem to thrive, just as your decreasing self-esteem contributes to more negative thoughts – round and round it goes.

Once you start paying attention to your thoughts, you will catch many self-esteem-damaging negative thoughts triggered by narcissistic abuse. Some include:

- Negative core beliefs: *"I am stupid." "I am no good." "I will never find love again."*

- Comparisons: *"I will never be as good as his current girlfriend."*

You might think your thoughts aren't affecting your self-esteem, but they are. Not all negative thoughts are obvious. Some subtle ones may erode your sense of self in more insidious ways.

A good example is blaming yourself when something goes wrong. *"If only I had left work earlier, I would have gotten home before my partner and he wouldn't have verbally assaulted me."*

This is you internalizing everything your narcissistic lover says about you and letting that define how you feel about yourself.

The question is, how can you stop negative thoughts from destroying your self-esteem?

First, you must identify the negative thoughts and beliefs you have. For example, if you often tell yourself, "I'm too stupid" or "I'm not worthy of love and affection," write down these negative beliefs in a journal or piece of paper.

Then, challenge these beliefs with facts. For example, *"I have many people asking me out on dates. I am worthy of love and affection."*

Next, write down positive things about yourself, specifically your good qualities and strengths. For example, *"I am thoughtful," "I am trustworthy,"* and *"I am easy to open up to."* Also, write down positive things that other people have said about you. Aim for five positive things and update the list as regularly as possible — perhaps every week.

Use the list or journal to remind yourself daily that the negative thoughts triggered by the narcissist's words don't define you or reflect your value.

Practice challenging and replacing your negative thoughts every day.

- **Repairing Your Self-Esteem**

The five strategies here will help you repair and rebuild your self-esteem after walking away from narcissistic abuse.

1. Self-Care

Self-care is great for your physical and mental health; it's an excellent way to show that you truly care about yourself. Spend more time with your loved ones, eat healthier diets, and do things you like. These are ways of reminding yourself that you deserve to be taken care of, healthy, and happy. You are worth the time and effort you invest in yourself.

Most victims of narcissistic abuse don't feel worthy of self-care after leaving a toxic relationship – but that shouldn't stop you from taking good care of yourself. Consistent self-care acts can rebuild your sense of self-worth and self-esteem.

Start by prioritizing and meeting your needs. If you feel like binge-shopping, do it. If you feel like stuffing your face with as much ice cream as possible, don't let anyone stop you. Invest in acts of self-care, no matter how small or trivial they may seem. The feelings of worthiness will naturally follow.

2. Connect with your core self

You cannot think highly of yourself if you can't even define who you are. In codependent relationships, the focus is always on meeting the narcissist's needs. Meanwhile, one person's needs remain unfulfilled.

When you focus on meeting someone else's needs and wants, it's easy to forget who you are, the things that matter to you, what you like, and so on. So, you will need to reconnect with your core self. In other words, remind yourself of who you truly are.

I encourage you to dedicate at least 30 minutes daily to connecting with your authentic self. You can do this with journaling and meditation. You can also try new things to see what you might like or return to hobbies the narcissists force you to abandon. See if you still enjoy or want to continue participating in those pleasurable activities.

3. Believe in yourself

It helps to know that you can trust yourself. Self-trust is integral to self-worth. You can start building your self-trust by keeping your promises to yourself. When you say you'll do something, be sure to do it. You must commit to your goals.

It's important to make your goals and commitment doable. Start with things you know you can accomplish easily – it'll help build your self-trust. Please don't set lofty goals that might be difficult to attain. Keep your goals simple and realistic.

For example, suppose you want to reduce your social media usage. You can start from 15 minutes instead of trying to stop altogether. When you reduce it by 15 minutes successfully, that's an accomplishment that will help you to build self-trust.

4. Tune in with your feelings

Feelings convey valuable information. For example, anxiety alerts you to a threat or danger, while resentment tells you someone is taking advantage of you. You must tune in with your feelings so your behavior can align accordingly.

Victims of narcissistic abuse often cope by suppressing their feelings. You may have stopped paying attention to how you feel completely. Or when you notice them, you don't do anything to meet your needs and address what the feeling is telling you. Therefore, you might need to practice intentionally paying attention to your feelings.

My favorite way of listening to my feelings is to tune in with my bodily sensations. You can try this too. Note how you feel when tired or hungry. Observe the bodily sensations you get when you're anxious or worried.

5. Practice assertiveness

Stand up for yourself. Assertiveness is a great way to rebuild your self-esteem. Setting boundaries is one of the ways you can become more assertive. I would say that practicing assertiveness is a form of self-care because it promotes your health and well-being and reinforces the value of your needs, wants, and opinions.

Assertiveness can be scary for someone just coming out of a toxic relationship. So, start by practicing with people you feel safe and comfortable around. These should be people who respect your opinions and tolerate disagreements.

Also, speak up about seemingly minor things and then build that up to more important boundaries. For example, speak up about what you want for dinner instead of going with whatever the other person says. It also helps to start saying "no" to small requests.

These tips will help you gain confidence as you set more important boundaries in your personal and professional relationships.

- **Finding Your Self-Worth**

Here are 10 steps you can take to find your self-worth again:

1. **Acknowledge the things you're good at.** Overcome the feeling of inadequacy triggered by narcissistic abuse by recognizing what you're good at. You may not feel like that at the moment, but these things exist. Participating in a new activity every week is a good strategy to help you recognize them. It could be singing, cooking, hiking, solving puzzles, or lifting weights.

2. **Seek more positive relationships.** Surround yourself with people who appreciate, admire, respect, and support you. These should be people who listen to your opinions and needs and show that they care about you. Building positive relationships with positive-minded people will help you find your self-worth again.

3. **Be kind to yourself and others.** Don't blame yourself for the narcissist's actions. Don't be self-critical. Instead, be kind and compassionate toward yourself. Hold yourself accountable and be responsible for your well-being. But don't ever blame yourself for the abuse you endured. How we treat

others is usually a reflection of how we perceive ourselves. So, ensure you treat everyone else kindly, too.

4. **Say "no" more regularly.** Don't agree to things you don't want to do. Overcome the urge to always say "yes" to people. Learn to prioritize your thoughts, feelings, wants, and needs. It's normal to be afraid of saying "no" to people you care about but do it anyway. People who genuinely respect you won't cut you off simply because you rejected them. Rather, they will respect your established boundaries.

5. **Challenge yourself more often.** Try new things. Explore new adventures. Do things that you ordinarily would be afraid of doing. Put yourself in situations that challenge you positively. This will remind you of what you're capable of. Challenges are a reminder that you can face and overcome adversities.

6. **Celebrate yourself.** No matter how small an achievement or success might seem, intentionally celebrate it. It is one of the best ways to improve how you feel about yourself.

To heal from narcissistic abuse, you must rebuild your self-esteem and find your self-worth again. Use the tips here to rediscover who you truly are.

Step Five Takeaway

- Narcissistic abuse can destroy your sense of self and self-worth, but you can rediscover yourself.

- A narcissist will use harsh words, insults, and criticism to make you feel bad and weaken your self-esteem. Remind yourself that their words don't describe you.

- Negative thinking patterns can further damage your self-esteem and self-worth. Identify and challenge your negative thoughts. Then, replace them with more positive thoughts.

- Rediscover your self-worth by participating in activities that you truly enjoy.

Step Six:

Change Your Environment

"I wish that people would stop destroying other people just because they were once destroyed."

- *Karen Salmansohn*

Our environment dictates how we will behave. If you live in a bad neighborhood, you'll always be on the watch for crime. Yes, crime can happen in good neighborhoods too, but the chances are significantly less compared to bad neighborhoods.

Environment plays an important role when healing from a toxic relationship. The wrong settings will make it much harder to accomplish. Healing cannot begin unless you disconnect from your narcissist, emotionally and physically.

It's impossible to heal in an unsafe environment. Think of a narcissistic relationship as a room with a putrid smell. At first, you catch a whiff of the smell. You may even point it out or try to make it go. But the longer you remain in the room, the more you get used to the smell. Eventually, you may not recognize the smell (or yourself) anymore.

Then, you make it out of this room. When you get out, you will realize just how miserable and trapped that environment made you. Many have been in narcissistic relationships for as long as 20 years, reminiscing on the good old days and waiting for that person they fell in love with to return. They know this person once existed, so they wait.

Healing begins with eliminating the threat. You must physically remove yourself from the environment created by the narcissist. More importantly, you must go no-contact or reduce contact to the minimum if there's no other way around it.

But changing the environment isn't just about physically leaving the narcissist and the relationship. Other things are involved in changing your environment to heal from narcissistic abuse. And that's what we'll be discussing in this chapter.

This chapter will teach you how to create an environment that increases your chances of breaking free and moving on from toxicity.

- **Create New Rituals**

Our daily habits shape our future. The things we repeatedly do defines who we become. These are our rituals. I'm not referring to religious or esoteric practices. Rather, I'm talking about the practical ritual that makes you feel in charge.

As the great philosopher Aristotle said, *"We are what we repeatedly do. Excellence, then, is not an act but a habit."*

I couldn't agree more. Forming healthy routines is the best way to go if you want to regain control and balance. Rituals are an excellent way to regain a much-needed sense of control if you're trying to move from a narcissistic relationship. When you're uncertain or dealing with anxiety about the future, rituals help you to focus and boost your confidence.

You may not realize it, but they will contribute significantly to your recovery by turning small, daily actions into major, life-changing ones. They will add meaning and joy to your new life.

Incorporating these new habits into your everyday life may feel challenging at first. Do not set unrealistic goals or try to get there overnight. Building rituals that nourish you, your desires, and your goals will take time and consistency. So, I have come up with a list of things you can do to make the process easier and more enjoyable.

- **Start small and build your way up.**

Do not start by biting off more than you can chew. This will only make you feel overwhelmed, which can push you to give up on recovering. It's best to start with one ritual, i.e., one goal, and start small.

If your priority is relieving your anxiety, choose a ritual like meditation, and begin with five minutes daily. Continue until that comes easily to you, then increase the length of meditation. Do this until you start practicing for up to 30 minutes daily.

At the same time, you can add another activity, like yoga, into the mix. Starting small is a surefire way to build a lasting foundation. This ensures you get long-term success, so don't try to form this new habit overnight.

- **Be kind to yourself.**

There will be days when you won't check off your to-do list or engage in new rituals. You must show yourself grace and kindness on days like this as you work on incorporating meaningful acts into your everyday routine.

Do your best and leave the rest. Take this as an opportunity to practice self-compassion. Be as gentle on yourself as you would on a kid trying something new for the first time. Be patient and focus on your healing.

- **Choose things that you enjoy.**

If you find that you're anxious to engage in the rituals you choose, or they feel impossible to adhere to – you may have to rethink them. These activities you choose should be things that you enjoy. Don't do things because you think you should. Instead, do them because they serve you.

Lightness and joy are key aspects of self-care. And choosing healthy rituals that you enjoy and look forward to is a key part of your journey. Suppose meditating at a specific time doesn't work for you; consider doing it at another time. If you don't like working out indoors, move outside. If you don't like painting, try journaling.

Find activities that nourish your mind, body, and soul – that you enjoy and look forward to.

Next, I have assembled a list of basic yet effective rituals you can start practicing today. The best thing about these routines is that you can do them easily at home. Following a morning routine is a great way to enhance your concentration and mood. It energizes you to face whatever challenge life brings during the day.

So, let's start with some rituals you can use to start your morning every day.

- Begin the day with yoga. It has plenty of physical and emotional benefits that we can't ignore. By turning yoga practice into a morning routine, you're making sure to start your day by uniting your body, soul, and mind. There's arguably nothing better than that.

- Eat healthily. I'm not saying you should have a complicated, tasking meal every morning. Rather, I'm saying you should ensure your morning meals give you the nutrients and vitamins needed to nourish your body and mind. Not only will eating healthy strengthen your immune system, but it will also make you feel better.

- Meditate. You might think, "I can't just sit still for 30 minutes doing nothing." But meditation isn't "doing nothing." Of course, not everyone can meditate for that long. Ten minutes is typically sufficient for most people to get the mind-calming and balancing benefits of meditation.

Part of your new rituals should include creating a daily self-care routine. You need to keep your social battery charged if you don't want to withdraw and recoil from your abuser. Self-massage is an excellent way to get your blood flowing and reduce your stress levels daily.

Then, you should have a nightly routine. Engaging in uplifting activities before bed can help to improve your sleep quality. That will, in turn, improve your overall health. A good night routine may include reading a few chapters from a good book. Reading is much better for your mood and mental health than watching TV. It's a great way to relax your body and mind.

You can also make it a nightly practice to write in your gratitude journal. Write a few things reminding yourself of what you're grateful for before bedtime. It's a sure way to go to bed with a positive mindset, meaning you'll also wake up with a positive attitude.

Do this daily to remind yourself that each day offers you an opportunity for a fresh start, and you must seize it for complete healing and recovery.

- **Avoid Social Media**

What do you do when you wake up first thing in the morning? You probably check your Twitter, Facebook, TikTok, or Instagram feed. There are so many things to see on your social media accounts... a photo or clip of someone's adorable puppy, a video of someone's engagement party, someone's promotion post, and probably tweets about the latest episode of Stranger Things.

You might consider this harmless. After all, social media is a way to connect to the world. Unfortunately, social media can be dangerous if you're in recovery from abuse.

One thing you might have noticed about social media is that everyone is an expert on every subject conceivable. This causes an information overload for social media users. You're likely to get bombarded about anything and everything – good or bad.

Staying updated about happenings worldwide is good, but you don't want to be privy to everything wrong with the lives of people you may not even know. It can lead to negativity overload, which can amplify anxiety, shame, depression, and other emotions you may struggle with in the wake of leaving your narcissistic abuser.

Another thing about social media is that it causes sleep deprivation. You might be scrolling through your feed a few months into your recovery journey. Just like that, you see a picture your toxic ex posted with their new fiancée. Before you know it, you're deep into the fiancée's media, watching clips of her cat with your ex's reflection in the mirror.

You might not necessarily relapse, but social media can make you lose focus. Not only can it disrupt your journey, but it can also disrupt your sleep schedule. That can diminish your sleep quality. As I've established, sleep is a vital part of the recovery process and integral to your overall health.

One can easily get lost in social media, forgetting it is real. For instance, people on Instagram tend to post photos of them living their best life. You might have a couple with several photos and videos that depict a seemingly loving relationship. But the thing is, many of these pictures are staged.

Instagram posts might suggest that someone's life is perfect when, in fact, it's far from that. This may lead to comparisons on your part. Comparing yourself to strangers on social media is unrealistic and harmful to your recovery and overall health. It can deplete your self-esteem and trigger or amplify feelings of anxiety and depression.

Social media may harm your recovery, but it's also a great way to stay connected. The support and sense of belonging that come from joining communities of survivors are why you must find ways to regulate your social media use. Do not avoid it completely.

Here are some tips you might find helpful:

- Reduce the time you spend online significantly. Don't spend too much time on your phone. Cut down your usage to one hour per day.

- Cut ties with anyone from your past. Purge your accounts of people who don't support your decision to leave the abusive relationship. This is an important part of recovery.

- Start your day with the morning routines we discussed instead of going straight to your phone when you wake up. Wait till the afternoon or nighttime to use your social media.

- Find communities for abuse survivors and people in recovery. That way, you can have an online support network without risking your recovery.

- Stay off social media platforms completely if you ever feel overwhelmed.

- **Avoid Negative People**

Negative people tend to cause problems for people everywhere they go. It's important to identify the negative individuals in your life and get rid of them immediately. More importantly, you must stop attracting negative and toxic people.

Without knowing it, you might give toxic people power over your thoughts, feelings, and behavior. So, I have some tips to help you regain your power and reduce the impact of toxic and negative individuals in your life.

- **Protect your time.**

Toxic people are vampires. They will try to monopolize your time, but you shouldn't give them that power. You might spend two hours worrying about a one-hour lunch with a toxic friend. If you spend another two hours venting to someone else after lunch, that's five hours. That means you've devoted five precious hours to that person's toxicity.

Do not let toxic people steal your time and energy. Invest your time into things you find pleasurable. Ensure that the negative individual gets the least of your time and energy. Deprive them of the attention they crave so much from you.

- **Dictate your attitude.**

The fastest way to ruin your mood is to spend time with toxic people. Their attitude can affect how you feel. Allowing a toxic individual to dictate how you feel gives them too much power. Consciously dictate your attitude. Make it a habit to stay positive despite the negative person's attitude or behavior.

- **Refocus yourself.**

Negative people can influence what you think about and how you behave. For instance, a know-it-all colleague might make it hard for you to contribute productively in a meeting. Notice how your thoughts and behavior change around toxic people. Then, consciously decide to decrease the energy you expend on them.

- **Spend time with positive people.**

Your recovery journey will be much harder if you surround yourself with negativity. So, instead, make friends with positive people to achieve and maintain balance. Positive people can brighten your spirit. Seek more positive people to include in your life and spend time with them regularly. Perhaps a date with a cheerful friend or a hangout that's sure to be vibrant with laughter. It'll help you stay on track as you navigate the process.

- **Spend More Time With Positive People**

Surrounding yourself with positive people is one of the best ways to adopt a more positive attitude. This sounds simple enough, but attracting positive people can be dicey. It is hard for some people and easy for others.

When you get out of a toxic relationship, it can be hard to attract positive people. This is because you will be struggling with negative feelings that may repel people from you. The good news is you can take steps to attract positive people. It would be best if you change your mindset and attitude, which will benefit your recovery in many ways.

The steps you'll take include getting out there and fact-checking your thoughts. Once you learn to do these, you'll form the habit, and it'll come to you naturally.

Spending time with positive people will benefit you in many ways, such as:

- Helping you to make better decisions

- Increasing your happiness

- Inspiring you to make positive changes in your life

- Giving you hope and excitement for your journey

So, how do you attract positive people?

- Repeat positive affirmations daily.

- Get rid of toxic people from your life.

- Practice gratitude daily – even for the most mundane things.

- Leave your comfort zone. Attend more social events and experience new people.

- Be flexible with your schedule.

- Help others and be kind.

- Do not be judgmental or critical of other people.

- Always tell the truth.

- Practice mindfulness in everything you do.

To fill your life with positivity, you must increase your exposure to people with the qualities you want. Surrounding yourself with positive people will be life-changing for you.

Step Six Takeaway

- Your environment is a big part of your healing and recovery journey. It would be best if you created the ideal environment to promote your emotional and mental well-being.

- Creating new rituals can help you regain control and rediscover who you are. Form new daily, morning, and nightly routines as you work toward recovery.

- Reduce your social media usage to avoid getting overwhelmed by negativity and information overload. It will help your journey.

- Eliminate toxic and negative people from your life and seek positive people to infuse your life with the positive energy needed to heal and move forward.

Step Seven:

Find Yourself Again

"The narcissist is like a bucket with a hole in the bottom: No matter how much you put in, you can never fill it up. The phrase "I never feel like I am enough" is the mantra of the person in the narcissistic relationship. That's because to your narcissistic partner, you are not. No one is. Nothing is."

- Dr. Ramani Durvasula

Many survivors of narcissistic abuse sacrifice their identities. Once they start experiencing abuse, they feel somewhat hollow – no idea who they are and what they like. If this applies to you, it's time to rediscover yourself. So, let's see how you can benefit from rediscovering who you truly are.

- **Deal with Feelings of Failure, Shame, Guilt, Self-Pity, and Depression**

I often remind people working through narcissistic abuse recovery that a key part of the process is working hard to unlearn behaviors that no longer serve them. One way to do that is to deal with negative feelings that arise during the process, including shame, guilt, self-pity, depression, and a sense of failure.

It's normal for feelings of failure to arise after you exit an abusive relationship. You might think, "I could have done more to make the relationship work." This feeling can lead to depression, which, in turn, brings up feelings of shame, guilt, and self-pity.

Toxic shame makes you feel like you're worthless. It happens when someone else treats you poorly, and you internalize that treatment, believing they were right to treat you that way. Toxic shame can make you feel worthless and useless or, in some cases, not as good as others.

Feeling of shame and self-pity arises when you believe you aren't good enough, usually because a narcissistic parent or partner keeps saying you aren't. This emotion hits your self-esteem and confidence badly, impairing how you see yourself.

At the same time, you may struggle with self-pity if you keep wondering why the abuse happened to you. Most people deal with some form of self-pity in the face of adversity. It's feeling sorry for yourself.

Self-pity is often confused with depression, but they are distinct feelings. Most people with depression tend to feel pity for themselves from time to time. However, self-pity stemming from depression is usually an emotional response to the symptoms of despair and emptiness that accompany depression. It's also possible to feel self-pity without being depressed.

These emotions are usually co-occurring in survivors of narcissistic abuse. So, you might contend with some or all of them. The problem with these negative feelings is that they can make it hard or impossible to see past your ordeal to the present moment and what awaits you in the future. That is why you must deal with them as they arise – to ensure they don't impede your healing and recovery journey.

Self-compassion is the key to overcoming these toxic feelings and changing how you feel about yourself. Pair this with self-awareness and mindfulness, and you're good to go. Many wrongly assume that self-compassion is an emotion. I'm afraid that's not right.

Self-compassion is a skill that you can learn and sharpen as you move through life. Fostering self-compassion is one of the most important things you must work on during recovery. It is essential.

While showing compassion to others is often easy, you may find it hard to extend that compassion toward yourself – especially after leaving a narcissistic ex. Instead, you may deal with self-blaming, self-shaming, and guilt.

But what does "self-compassion" entail?

Compassion is broadly described as "an awareness of the distress that others are experiencing and a desire to help." I see self-compassion as the application of this same sentiment to oneself.

Every survivor needs support through their healing and recovery journey. And why shouldn't you find that support from within?

Don't think of self-compassion as a destination or milestone you must attain. Instead, think of it as a tool in your journey to healing and growth – a medium to help you achieve this. That said, self-compassion isn't easy to foster.

The good news is I have three vital but simple steps that you must take to start exploring and fostering self-compassion.

1. **Use positive affirmations to foster self-compassion.**

An absence of self-compassion is usually marked by the shame monster – the voice in your head that pops up randomly at will. This shame monster often repeats phrases such as:

- "I'm not good enough."
- "I should have; could have."
- "I made the wrong decision. I shouldn't feel this way."

As I said, cultivating self-compassion is a skill. So, just as you would when learning a new skill, you must practice by "talking back" to that voice in your head. And you must make sure that your inner voice is stronger, louder, and more powerful than the voice of the shame monster. An excellent way to "talk back" is to use positive affirmations.

Examples to try include:

- "I am worthy."
- "I am good enough."
- "I am absolutely deserving of love."

- "I am unique in my own ways."

- "My feelings are valid – I am allowed to feel this way."

You can write down some personal affirmations that apply specifically to you and your situation in a journal and repeat them in front of the mirror every morning to boost self-confidence.

2. **Realign with your body.**

Remember what I said about somatic therapy, which focuses on the connection between the mind and body? Well, I invite you to use this to realign your mind with your body. Using drawing as a tool for processing helps, especially because it allows you to express yourself from a mental space you never knew was accessible.

With this in mind, realign your body and mind by drawing how it feels to lean into the positive affirmations I listed above or the ones you come up with. Try focusing on the ones that speak deeply to you.

Use any creation mediums and colors that resonate with you in the process. As you do this, please pay attention to how drawing feels. Notice tensed areas in your body and try releasing the tension through your art.

3. **Move.**

Express yourself through movements that resonate with you. For instance, if you need to process feelings of failure or self-pity, you might try yoga poses that alternate between opening and closing. These might help you feel unstuck.

Self-compassion isn't easy to foster, particularly because you're probably your worst critic. So, you will find it incredibly helpful to use these tips to help you access and deal with toxic feelings.

Don't judge yourself for feeling how you feel. An important part of the process is releasing the judgment you or others have placed on you. With time, you will find this empowering.

- **Stop Attracting Abusers**

Let's say you're starting to rediscover yourself and believe it's time to re-enter the dating pool. In that case, how can you ensure that you don't attract another abuser? After all, you don't want to repeat the same mistake – no more narcissists or abusers!

How do you stop attracting abusers?

Again, the most important step you can take is to set firm boundaries and enforce them. It's kind to be empathetic and giving, but you don't want to be exploited and taken advantage of. Avoid this by firmly establishing and enforcing boundaries.

Next, you must work on building up your confidence. Do not tolerate anyone who makes you feel less than others. Building your confidence is a lifelong journey, but you can start now. Remind yourself of the things you deserve – and let that self-confidence shine. This will show any prospective abusers that you aren't prey or someone to be easily manipulated.

Additionally, always hone in on people's values. An individual's values are a true reflection of who they are. Connect with people based on their morals and values. More importantly, look for objective facts that support these so-called values. And finally, use your gut.

Narcissists lack empathy, and they can't even fake it. You can usually sense if an individual truly connects with you or not.

It also helps to watch out for red flags. Narcissists' personalities tend to fluctuate depending on the situation. Their public persona is different from their private persona. Pay attention to how an individual treats you publicly versus privately in the early phases of your relationship.

While you might be tempted to brush off any red flags, especially if the person treats other people so well, go with your gut and take action as soon as the red flags show up. A healthy relationship shouldn't make you feel like there's something off – believe in yourself if you think something is off.

Finally, stay away from people who try to control your behavior. Suppose you notice that this new person imposes their opinions on you and becomes irritated when you don't agree. In that case, exit the relationship before it goes any further. Attempting to control others' behavior or mold them into a desirable version is how abuse often starts.

A healthy partner will accept you for who you are instead of trying to change you or make your own decisions.

The more you familiarize yourself with the signs of narcissism and who narcissists tend to go for, the easier it becomes to avoid narcissists.

- **Practice Self-Love (The Greatest Form of Love)**

Before you can practice self-love, you must understand what it means. Self-love is a sense of appreciation for yourself. It grows when you engage in actions that promote your physical, mental, emotional, and spiritual well-being.

Practicing self-love means putting a great value on your happiness and well-being. It means prioritizing your needs without sacrificing your well-being for others. Self-love means not settling for less.

I like to think self-love is subjective; it means different things to everyone. We all have different ways we want to take care of ourselves. As a result, the first step to practicing self-love is determining what it looks like for you.

For you, self-love could mean:

- Prioritizing your needs and wants
- Talking about yourself with kindness
- Being true to your values
- Trusting yourself
- Being kind to yourself
- Taking a break from self-criticism and self-judgment
- Setting firm boundaries
- Allow yourself to make mistakes

- Forgiving yourself for making mistakes

- Not comparing yourself to others

- Not worrying about people's opinions or perceptions of you

- Reminding yourself that your value isn't based on your body or looks

- Letting go of toxic people

- Believing in your ability to make decisions that are right for you

- Creating your opportunities and taking whichever life throws at you

- Embracing your emotions as fully as you can

We could say that self-love is the same as self-care. Practicing self-care requires you to:

- Listen to your body

- Take breaks from work to move or stretch your body

- Put your phone down and connect to nature by going outdoors

- Do something fun and creative

- Eat healthily and sometimes indulge your cravings

Self-love means embracing yourself at this moment for what you are. It means embracing your emotions and prioritizing your physical and psychological well-being.

My favorite thing about self-love is that it encourages us to make healthier choices. When you hold yourself in high regard, you will make choices that nourish and serve you well. This may be exercising, eating healthy, and forming healthy bonds.

Here are some ideas to help you practice self-love:

- Becoming more mindful of your thoughts, feelings, wants, and needs.

- Take action based on what you need rather than what you want. Focusing on your needs steers you away from problematic behavioral patterns that can deplete your self-love.

- Practice good self-care. Self-love comes naturally when you take care of your basic needs. Nourish yourself with healthy activities, such as proper sleep, good nutrition, exercise, and healthy social and intimate interactions.

- Cultivate healthy habits. Show that you truly care for yourself through what you engage in. Don't do things just because you have to get them done. Instead, do them because you care about what they'll do for you.

Finally, start being patient, gentle, kind, and compassionate to yourself as you would with people you care about.

As you work on rediscovering yourself, you may not feel particularly powerful after leaving a narcissistic relationship. In moments where you feel incredibly down, remind yourself of what you survived and how far you've come.

Self-love won't happen overnight, but it will settle in your mind with time.

- **Prioritizing Self-Care**

Prioritizing self-care is the key to living a balanced, smooth, and effective life. It ensures you can bring your best to whatever challenges or adversities. Here are my top tips to help you prioritize self-care:

- Dedicate 30 minutes every day to you. Use that time to focus on yourself only. You might think this will affect your productivity, but it will boost it. Use this time to connect with yourself and determine what you need. You can write in your journal, walk in the park, meditate, or practice mindfulness.

- Be realistic with your goals and to-do list. Every day, identify three things you intend to achieve. Then, break these down into small, actionable steps. You will make progress and get that needed sense of achievement.

- Watch your internal language. Listen to how you speak to or about yourself. Make it a point to speak to yourself how you would talk to a best friend on their worst day.

- Recognize and focus on the things that matter.

Self-care isn't selfish. Tending to your needs is the best gift you can give to yourself and everyone else in your life.

Step Seven Takeaway

- Finding yourself again means discarding the idea of who others think you should be and embracing the real, authentic you. It means rediscovering your values and morals.

- Narcissists can sense when someone would make a good victim to prey on. Build up your confidence to show prospective abusers that you aren't to be trifled with.

- Find new ways to practice self-love and self-care each day.

Step Eight:

Seek Support

"Narcissists would rather lie and humiliate you than to admit that they were in the wrong."

- Mitta Xinindlu

Leaving a narcissistic partner isn't going to be easy; it will be a heavy burden on you. There might be times when you will feel alone and empty without your narcissistic ex and times when you will feel a strong urge to go back to them. But doing that would be a huge step backward, which is why you must have people you can reach out to and rely on for strength and encouragement in those moments.

These people should make up your support network and be able to offer the mental and emotional strength you need to remain firm and overcome moments of weakness and difficult times.

- **Why You Need External Support**

Leaving a narcissistic relationship is one of the biggest decisions you'll ever make. It will impact your health and future significantly. Recovery will require you to acquire new thinking and behavioral patterns. Therefore, it can be isolating to an extent.

You may find it challenging to open up and seek support from your loved ones. Shame and social stigma may also hinder you from asking for help. However, it would help if you had an understanding, compassionate support system to positively impact your healing and recovery.

A support system refers to a group of people who can offer you social and practical processes during and after your healing journey. Support systems are typically categorized into two: those geared toward recovery and those composed of personal relationships.

Your support system may include the following:

- Family members

- Friends or peers

- Neighbors

- Members of your church, club, or other organizations

For your support system, you may go to the people in your life whom you trust, including family and friends.

On the other hand, your recovery support system should be a group designed specifically for survivors of narcissistic abuse or abuse in general, as well as those in recovery. The meetings may be in-person or virtual.

If you can't establish a strong personal support system, it is OK to use recovery support systems when actively trying to recover. But if you can, you may join a recovery support group after the hard part is over.

You might wonder how having external support can help. Well, if you're in recovery or beyond, having a support system will help keep you balanced in a few ways.

First, being in a narcissistic relationship can be isolating. The narcissist isolates you from your loved ones, affecting your relationship. Reconnecting with family and friends after leaving an abusive relationship can signify the start of a new chapter in your life. For example, you may take it as an opportunity to repair all relationships impaired by your ex.

But you may have been encouraged by the people in your life to stay in the relationship, which is a different ball game. That is why you need a healthy support network during recovery. It can make a significant difference.

External support also helps because surrounding yourself with people who positively impact you is the best thing you can do during recovery.

- **Rely on Peer Support**

Peer support is one of the best tools you should have during recovery. It comes in different forms, but peer support generally involves giving and receiving support from people who have been in the same situation as you.

It could be sharing knowledge or exchanging emotional support, interpersonal interactions, and practical help. In a peer support group, your experiences are just as important as anybody else's. And no one's opinion is more important than anyone else.

You will give and receive support depending on what you need at different times. It's all about what you feel is right. Studies have shown that peer support can help to improve a person's well-being. It is an effective tool for accessing a larger support pool and building your self-esteem, confidence, and interpersonal skills.

Some types of peer support include:

- Support or self-help groups: These comprise trained peers. Members focus on exchanging emotional support and information and sharing experiences. They also engage in many practical activities to make the process easier.

- One-to-one support: This is also called befriending or mentoring. You're assigned an individual with whom you can meet to discuss your thoughts and feelings and set goals together.

- Virtual groups and online forums.

Peer support can happen face-to-face, digitally, or via the phone. You can make it weekly, monthly, ongoing, or limited. It all depends on what you need.

Find a peer support group via NHS services. You can speak to your doctor or healthcare professional about this. Some mental health groups also offer peer support. Check the local directory to figure out what's available in your area.

Before seeking peer support, you must determine if it's right for you. It's normal to experience anxiety about opening up to strangers. You may find it difficult to share your experiences with others.

Remember that most people in your community feel the same way as you do or feel at some point. It's entirely your prerogative to choose how much you want to share with the people in your group.

Focus on how you're feeling during the meeting. Can you cope with listening to other people share experiences that hit so close to home? While you may find it helpful to hear how other survivors have coped, it's normal to initially find the process triggering or upsetting.

Peer support is not the same as the help you get from a therapist because the latter is more tailored to you. Remember that people will share their experiences and strategies; just because something worked for one member doesn't mean it will work for you.

Figure out what you want from peer support. Different groups offer different approaches. For example, suppose you don't want to be in a group that requires you to sit and discuss your feelings. In that case, you can join a group that focuses on activities instead.

It's OK if peer support doesn't help you. That doesn't mean you were wrong to try. It probably just means that wasn't the right kind of support for you. So, consider trying again in the future.

- **Seek Professional Help for Narcissistic Abuse Recovery**

Reaching out for professional help can take a lot of courage. Thankfully, help is available. Usually, the first step toward making a positive change is meeting with a therapist. If you'd prefer to see a mental health provider alone, you might opt for individual therapy.

Many therapists are specialized in abuse recovery. They can help you rebuild your self-esteem and autonomy. If you experienced gaslighting during your relationship, a professional could help you restore trust in your emotions and memories.

Suppose you begin therapy while still in the relationship. In that case, you may work with your therapist to hatch an escape plan to exit the relationship in the most hassle-free way possible. After you leave the relationship, you're likely to have PTSD from emotional abuse.

Fortunately, there are different types of therapy a professional can help you explore during recovery. For instance, Eye Movement Desensitization and Reprocessing (EMDR) is a form of therapy to help abuse survivors unlock memories blocked in the mind so they can begin healing.

Your therapist might recommend journal therapy to help you deal with the psychological effects of abuse. Or they might help you process your feelings through physical sensations using somatic experiences.

After your first visit to a mental health provider, your therapist will customize treatment according to what they think you need and what will be effective for your situation.

Group therapy is commonly recommended to survivors of narcissistic abuse. It comprises survivors who share their memories and feelings. Meeting other people in similar situations can help reduce shame and isolation.

Therapy encourages open communication, creating a safe and positive space to rebuild your self-esteem and confidence.

Recovering from the trauma of narcissistic abuse can be difficult and take a long time. Seeking professional help will benefit you throughout the healing process. Lifestyle changes also impact the process significantly.

As I've reiterated a few times, narcissistic abuse tends to cause physical and psychological health concerns. Self-care is one of the most powerful tools to have during recovery. Combine self-care with therapy, and you're on to a good thing.

A healthy diet, exercise, and good sleep habits are enough to boost your mood and overall well-being. It also helps to have a daily routine of leisure activities and healthy hobbies.

- **How to Find a Therapist**

When finding a licensed therapist, you must consult local resources, organizations, apps, and trusted online therapy options. What do you need to know about finding the right therapist for you? Find out everything below.

If you're thinking about seeking individual professional help to recover from the trauma of abuse, finding the right therapist is your first hurdle. The bond between a therapist and their patient is extremely important. It can impact your growth positively or negatively.

That is why you must research, ask important questions, and pay close attention to finding the right therapist.

Next are some tips for finding a therapist to help you in your journey toward narcissistic abuse recovery.

- **Consult your insurance provider directory.**

If you intend to make therapy treatments via your insurance plan, then your first step is to look through your provider's network. You should also see if your plan limits the number of sessions you can attend annually and whether you'll have to pay out of pocket if you choose an out-of-network therapist.

- **Talk to people you trust.**

Referrals are a great way to find a therapist who would make a good fit for you. Speak to a friend, coworker, or medical practitioner that you trust. While referrals are great, you should also know that people have different therapy needs and goals. So, just because a therapist is a great match for someone you know doesn't mean they will be as beneficial to you.

- **Search reputable online databases.**

Many mental health organizations and groups run up-to-date, accessible databases of professional mental help providers. This could be as easy as entering your ZIP code in the database and getting a list of licensed therapists in your local area. You may even look up specialists, such as counselors or therapists, who focus on narcissistic abuse recovery.

Examples of online search tools to try are:

- American Psychological Association
- American Association of Marriage and Family Therapists
- Mayo Clinic
- Association of LGBTQ+ Psychiatrists

- **Try local resources.**

Your local community may have helpful resources. For example, your school may give you access to a counselor or counseling center if you're a student. Suppose you're employed. In that case, your company's HR team may offer a list of therapists accessible via an employee assistance program or workplace wellness.

- **Explore organizations that address your specific concern.**

Since you'd be looking for a therapist to help specifically with narcissistic abuse recovery, you might search for therapists via a helpline, network, or national association. Many professional organizations provide resources to help you find mental health providers that address your area of concern. For example, the International Association of Firefighters provides resources for Post-Traumatic Stress Disorder.

- **Identify your goals before therapy.**

What are your therapy goals? What do you hope to accomplish? Think of this ahead of time when you and your therapist both have the same goals, the chances of success increase exponentially.

If you think you might need some medication to cope with the after-effects of abuse, you should go for a therapist who is open to prescribing medications.

If you want to join a community of people with similar experiences, you should look for a therapist who works with support groups or offers group therapy sessions.

Know that it's OK if your goals change as you work toward recovery. Speak to your therapist about modifying your treatment plan as your needs and goals evolve.

- **Explore online therapy apps.**

BetterHelp and Talkspace are two of the most popular online therapy tools to help you find the kind of therapist you want. You can work with the licensed, accredited professional they match with you via phone or virtually.

Many people are more comfortable with digital therapy than in-person therapy. Plus, the former is more cost-effective.

- **How to Find a Narcissistic Abuse Support Group**

A narcissistic abuse support group is a safe environment where you can meet with other survivors to support one another as you heal from the traumatic experiences you've been subjected to. There are peer-led groups and others led by licensed therapists. Peer-led narcissistic abuse support groups usually rotate leadership among members of the group.

These groups are a safe space where you can find listening ears, validation, and support from others who share your experience. They are more effective when combined with psychotherapy and can be a key part of your healing journey.

There are different ways to find a narcissistic abuse support group. First, speak to your mental health provider and ask if they can refer you to any narcissistic abuse support group in your area. They can share information with you or point you in the right direction.

Some resources that may also help you include:

- National Domestic Violence Hotline

- Help Within Reach

- I Believe Your Abuse

Seeking external support from your peers, community, and mental health professionals can make a huge impact as you work on recovering from abuse and rebuilding healthy relationships.

Step Eight Takeaway

- Complete isolation is a huge component of narcissistic abuse. External support is critical as you navigate healing and recovery.

- Listening to others share their experiences and how they overcame narcissistic abuse can help you realize that you aren't alone and that it is easy to move forward.

- Online therapy is equally as helpful as in-person therapy; what matters is your needs.

- Therapy is more likely to succeed if your goals align with your therapist's. So, be sure to set your goals ahead of time.

- Find a community of narcissistic abuse survivors to make the process easier and reduce negative feelings that arise during recovery.

Step Nine:

On The Road To Recovery After A Toxic Relationship

"To love oneself is the beginning of a life-long romance."

- Oscar Wilde

Undoubtedly, the road to joy and happiness after a traumatic experience can be a long but rewarding one. You will see yourself going through what feels like the most hellish days of your life. But look here – there is a bright light at the end of the tunnel. Your joyful days with lots of genuine smiles and happiness are here. Right now, happiness is the goal, and by applying the steps discussed so far, you should see every part of your life blossom.

While it's important that you look happy, it's crucial that you "feel" happy! Be genuinely happy from the inside to the outside. Then you can completely eliminate all the residues from your narcissistic relationship.

This final step will provide you with strategies to get on your road to recovery after abuse.

- **Signs That You Are Recovering From Abuse**

    1. **You tell yourself the truth**

It can be painful to know that someone you love could want to harm you. Armed with this perception, you will always blame yourself for your abuser's faults. *"I must have said something wrong," "I could have done things better," "I should have lost more weight."* These and many more thoughts are excuses you may give to justify the actions of your abuser because you love them to a fault.

Having been blinded by the narcissist's deception, you tend to see nothing wrong in how they mistreated you. But when you suddenly realize that they've not been fair in how you were treated all this while, and you now know you deserve better —Congratulations! Your recovery just began.

You now know you deserve better, and your heart needs to heal. You now view things more objectively and not with the eyes of "love." This is you being honest with yourself. For once, you are not making excuses for them – you have seen that you've been at the receiving end.

2. The experience saddens you

Having realized that the one you love so much has abused you and that you have lied to yourself for so long, chances are you will have a lot of emotions bottled up inside. This realization is a possible sign that recovery has begun.

So what should you do with all the bottled-up emotions struggling to burst from within? Allow them all to play out. These are likely mixed emotions of anger, regret, and sadness. Bottling them up can make you suffer trauma.

You will likely get angry for allowing yourself to suffer the actions of your abuser for that long. You may ask, "What was I thinking?" Then you'll regret ever investing so much into the relationship. You will also regret showing so much love and not reciprocating. You will end up sad about the experience. When you start experiencing these barrages of emotions, it's a possible sign of healing.

3. You are true to your emotions

For a long time, you masked your emotions. You lied to yourself that you were okay with being in a narcissistic relationship. That was probably your own way of getting by each day. You were afraid to express your emotions, and you suppressed them most of the time. And because of this, you could not confront the situation for a long time. However, if you can now let go of your emotions - get angry when you feel like it, or sad when you feel like it, and genuinely express your deep emotions – then you are healing. Being honest with yourself is a good sign of recovery.

4. You put yourself first

The narcissist's words, actions, and choices controlled you for a long while. You lived to please them and had no say about your well-being. But now, you think about what's best for you first and care less about the narcissist's opinion. You suddenly realize you have dreams and aspirations, hobbies and desires. You are making yourself a priority, and you love it! That's great because it means you are healing.

5. Improved physical health

When you go through a narcissistic relationship, you suffer many physical health problems such as body pains, headaches, stomach upsets, and lots more. When you free yourself from such toxicity, you are likely to experience an alleviation of these symptoms, and your physical health begins to improve. This renewed physical strength and absence of aches and pains are a sign that you are healing.

6. You start to reject condemnations

You have unconsciously lived your life with several negative comments and condemnations. You have unknowingly let them rule your mind for a long time while the abusive relationship lasted. With the narcissist leaving your life, you realize that such negative comments exist in your subconscious mind. You will most likely wonder how they got there in the first place! And then you somehow get the strength to prove them wrong.

7. You decide to let go

Forgiving yourself and the one that has hurt you is a clear sign that you are healing. That doesn't necessarily mean that you want to let the narcissist back into your life, nor do you deny that nothing happened. Forgiving, here, is a way of emancipating yourself from all the hurt that has kept you locked up while you suffered. It is a sign of strength. You are now rising above the situation that previously broke you.

8. You are more confident

You are now more confident in yourself and can make your own decisions. You are no longer restrained by the constant manipulation of the narcissist who previously talked down your every move and made you question your capabilities.

9. You can set your boundaries

When you see that you can now set boundaries in a relationship and not allow yourself to be bossed around and dictated to by the narcissist, you know you are healing.

10. You start to associate with people again

Narcissists keep you isolated for a long time because of their manipulative tactics of making you doubt your sanity. So for a long while, you couldn't trust people freely or even go out and have fun with people close to you. Now, you are coming alive and starting to socialize with people again. You find it easy to trust others.

- **People to Be Wary of When On a Date**

Now that you're healing and may want to consider dating, you may want to be more careful this time to avoid falling into the shackles of narcissists. To avoid being in a narcissistic relationship, you should be wary of specific people.

1. **Those who are late without an excuse**

It's normal to be late for a date sometimes due to traffic or other reasons. Your date should call to explain the situation and apologize for running late. When they finally arrive, they should be visibly sorry for keeping you waiting. That's an ideal situation. On the other hand, suppose your date runs unusually late and doesn't call to let you know they're on their way. In that case, they arrive late without explaining, and if this repeats itself again, that's a red flag! The person doesn't care about you, nor are they sensitive to your feelings.

2. **Those who expect too much from the onset**

Going on a date with someone expecting too much from you on a first date can be a warning sign that you may go into a narcissistic relationship. Perhaps, they want you to start avoiding the opposite sex, calling them by a pet name, and even limiting your movement. Such partners may not respect your opinion if you eventually get serious with them. You should boldly express your displeasure at such behaviors if they arise during the date. Also, don't allow them to impose themselves on you. You should be at liberty to decide if you want to go out again with them, and they should respect your decision.

3. Those who want to talk only about themselves

Being on a date allows you and the other party to get to know each other better. But when your date is only concerned about themselves and begins to talk endlessly about their lives to the extent of revealing very private matters too soon, that can be a red flag. There's every likelihood that such persons have a lot of emotional baggage, and the relationship will only serve as a platform to offload them. You or your feelings are never going to matter in such a situation.

4. The interviewer

Some dates can make you feel like you are facing a work panel! You sit across the table with the big boss facing you and cross-examining you! For Pete's sake, it's a date, not a job interview! If you're going to feel so uncomfortable answering all kinds of questions without the chance of having a proper relaxed conversation, then it's a big NO.

5. The very passive date

You and your date should be actively involved in planning the date. However, be wary of a partner not interested in any part of the planning - the place, the food, the time, etc. This isn't a good sign.

6. The absent-minded partner

You have to be wary of dates who are never present with you at the table because they have to attend to one issue or the other. Even when seated, their minds are far away. A proper and considerate date should be able to spare some time to relax and have some alone time with you.

7. The rude type

It's a bad sign if your date turns out to be rude to others, probably the doorman or waiter, on your first date. It shows that they are insensitive and don't place much value on others. If they do that to someone, they'll do the same to you someday.

8. The prejudiced

There's a common saying that "everyone is entitled to their opinions." If your date finds it hard to comprehend your opinion in a discussion and constantly tries to shove theirs down your throat, then you should be wary of them because your view will never count in such a relationship!

9. The Bitter Partner

It's okay to talk about previous relationships when on a date. However, when a partner expresses excessive bitterness over past relationships or their ex, that's a sign they're not quite over them yet. If they constantly blame their ex for everything, that's a possible sign they're not responsible either.

- **Steps To Ensure Abuse Doesn't Happen Again**

The best way to ensure a narcissist does not abuse you again is to change your mindset about yourself, others, and relationships. You can do this in the following ways:

1. **Change the way you think about yourself**

Change begins in your mind. Yes, you may have faced abuse before, which has affected your thought pattern. The narcissist may have manipulated you into thinking that you are worthless. If you must make it right this time, you must first change how you see yourself. Start loving yourself and know that you deserve to be loved.

2. **Change the way you think about others**

Stop thinking you can determine what others should do or how they should be in a relationship. You cannot control the other party. You can only be the best of yourself. Determined to succeed and be on top of any situation that may arise.

3. Rightly distinguish between love and obsession

Do not confuse your partner's obsession with you for love. Besides being in a relationship, you should have healthy relationships with others, like your family and friends. Don't be silent if your partner is suffocating you with obsessive attitudes and demands and denying you an identity outside the relationship. Speak up and walk away if need be.

4. Slow down and live life one day at a time

Your previous toxic relationship must have been with a partner who consistently placed you on edge. It would help if you learned to take things slowly now. Do not live life in a rush. Consider yourself and your well-being. Do not see your relationship as more extensive than what it is – a relationship. That is not to say you should subsequently be self-centered, but you should not take more than you can accommodate in pleasing your partner and being there for them.

5. Do not be afraid of being alone

Do not remain in a toxic relationship for the sake of being involved with someone or for fear of what others say. Choose your happiness over pleasing others.

- **Build Trust and Strengthen Future Relationships without Allowing Past Abuse to Affect Your Happiness**

You can surely love and be happy again after an abusive relationship. It may be challenging to go all out and start trusting again, but you can if you try. Use the following steps to achieve this.

1. Ensure that you have healed

Before entering a new healthy relationship where you can build trust with your new partner, you must have healed, forgiven yourself, and overcome the painful past. Be willing to start afresh.

2. Discuss the past with your new partner

Be open with your new partner about the toxicity you faced in the past and how the previous relationship has affected your self-esteem and ability to trust again. Also, state your willingness to contribute to the success of the new relationship. You aren't asking to be pitied, but it will help them understand and empathize with you.

3. Be patient with your new partner

It may be tempting to sometimes judge your new partner by the selfish behavior of your ex. You must understand that your partner is different from your ex. Be objective in ironing out issues with them.

4. Love your partner

Don't guard your heart against feeling and showing love. Be free with your partner and love them as you should. You deserve to love and be loved again.

5. Communication is key

Communicate freely with your partner. Loosen up and have healthy chats, laughs, and discussions with them, as that will make you quickly grow fond of each other.

Step Nine Takeaway

- Recovery starts when you are now honest with yourself, confident, true to your emotions, prioritize yourself, create boundaries, decide to let go, and associate with people again.

- When next you're on a date, be wary of people who are late without a reasonable excuse, self-centered people, rude people, absent-minded people, and those who don't value your opinions.

- Change how you see yourself and others to avoid being in a toxic relationship.

- Know the difference between love and obsession.

- Don't be afraid to be alone.

- Before starting a new relationship, ensure that you've healed, talk about your past experience, and prioritize communication.

Conclusion

"The only person that deserves a special place in your life is someone that never made you feel like you were an option in theirs."

- Shannon L. Alder

I want to reiterate that abuse is never the victim's fault. Narcissistic abuse can scramble your sense of reality, making you think that whatever you're going through currently or you've gone through is your fault. No matter what, know that it isn't your fault.

Narcissistic abuse can be damaging. Still, you can recover from it. Healing from the effects of narcissistic abuse can be challenging, frustrating, and lonely, but it is possible. While the process can be lengthy and complex, you can make it happen.

Throughout this book, I have outlined nine steps to overcome narcissistic abuse while you begin a healing and recovery journey. As I said in the book, healing begins with acknowledging the reality of your experience. Since the nature of this abuse is usually subtle, it may take a while before you can recognize and acknowledge that it happened.

If you've been constantly subjected to narcissistic abuse, you may experience long-term physical and mental effects. But take the necessary steps toward recovery, such as acknowledging the abuse, leaving the abuser, seeking professional help, and rediscovering yourself. You can heal from the trauma and move past the experience.

You may need years to fully recover from the damage done to you due to the narcissist's psychological manipulation and gaslighting. With that said, you can move past the abuse and achieve complete recovery with everything you learned in this book and professional help.

Good luck!

Exclusive 5-day bonus course just for you!

We will be sharing more tips, methods and topics that will help you cope with negative emotions, abusive relationships and many more so you can emerge stronger and better.

Simply let us know where to send the course e-mails to via this link below.

https://bit.ly/rowena-spring

For any general feedback & enquiries, you can reach us at bookgrowthpublishing@mail.com

Resources List

American Psychiatric Association. What are personality disorders? Retrieved from https://www.psychiatry.org/patients-families/personality-disorders/what-are-personality-disorders)

American Psychiatric Association. (2012). DSM-IV and DSM-5 Criteria for the Personality Disorders. Retrieved from https://www.nyu.edu/gsas/dept/philo/courses/materials/Narc.Pers.DSM.pdf

Arabi, S. (2020, May). The Truth About Dating After Narcissistic Abuse That Every Survivor Needs To Know. Retrieved from Thought Catalog: https://thoughtcatalog.com/shahida-arabi/2017/12/the-truth-about-dating-after-narcissistic-abuse-every-survivor-needs-to-know/

Audrey (Dr.) (2019) "How you can Help Yourself Heal" Medium Retrieved from https://medium.com/invisible-illness/how-you-can-help-yourself-heal-2290e8ebde8e

Brogaard, B. (2019, June). Vulnerable Vs Grandiose Narcissism: Which Is More Harmful? Retrieved from Psychology Today: https://www.psychologytoday.com/us/blog/the-mysteries-love/201906/vulnerable-vs-grandiose-narcissism-which-is-more-harmful

Brown, L. (2020, March). How To Deal With A Narcissist When You're Stuck At Home With Them. Retrieved from Hack Spirit: https://hackspirit.com/how-to-deal-with-narcissist/

Davis, J. (2017, July). Grandiose Narcissism VS Vulnerable Narcissism: What Are the Differences? Retrieved from Learning Mind: https://www.learning-mind.com/grandiose-narcissism-vulnerable-narcissism/

Caligor E, Levy KN, Yeomans FE. Narcissistic personality disorder: diagnostic and clinical challenges. (https://ajp.psychiatryonline.org/doi/full/10.1176/appi.ajp.2014.14060723#B11) Am J Psychiatry. 2015;172(5):415-22.

Coleman, N "Seven Steps to healing yourself" Mail Online Retrieved from https://www.dailymail.co.uk/health/article-85148/Seven-steps-healing-yourself.html

Corbett, M. (2019, May). Confident or narcissistic? Here are 5 ways to tell the difference. Retrieved from Thriveworks: https://thriveworks.com/blog/confident-or-narcissistic/

Craig, H. (2020, April). 10 Ways To Build Trust in a Relationship. Retrieved from Positive Psychology: https://positivepsychology.com/build-trust/

Elissa (2015) "6 Steps To Healing Yourself" Elissa Goodman Retrieved from https://elissagoodman.com/uncategorized/6-steps-to-healing-yourself/

Everyday Health (2017, November). Begin Your Journey Of Self Discovery. Retrieved from Everyday Health: https://www.everydayhealth.com/healthy-living/begin-your-journey-self-discovery/

Firestone, Lisa. (2013, May). In a Relationship with a Narcissist? What You Need to Know About Narcissistic Relationships. Retrieved from Psychalive: https://www.psychalive.org/narcissistic-relationships/

Garis, M.G (2020) '9 Things to Do After a Breakup That are actually Healthy and Healing" Well + Good Retrieved from https://www.wellandgood.com/things-to-do-after-a-breakup/

Globe Gazers(n.d). "13 Lessons on How to Recover From a Breakup the Healthy Way" Retrieved from https://www.globe-gazers.com/how-to-recover-from-a-breakup-healthy-way/

Grey, S. (n.d). Dating after Narcissistic Abuse: Red Flags and Sav's Dating Do's and Don'ts. Retrieved from Esteemology: https://esteemology.com/dating-after-narcissistic997/

HelpGuide.org. Narcissistic Personality Disorder. Retrieved from https://www.helpguide.org/articles/mental-disorders/narcissistic-personality-disorder.htm

Ishak, R. (2019) "How to find your confidence after a breakup" The Every Girl Retrieved from https://theeverygirl.com/how-to-find-confidence-after-a-breakup/

Lancer, D. (2019, May). Why Narcissists Act the Way They Do. Retrieved from Psych Central: https://psychcentral.com/lib/why-narcissists-act-the-way-they-do/

Legg, T. (2019, January). 11 Signs You're Dating a Narcissist — and How to Get Out. Retrieved from Healthline; https://www.healthline.com/health/mental-health/am-i-dating-a-narcissist#9

Mayo Clinic (2017, November). Narcissistic Personality Disorder. Retrieved from https://www.mayoclinic.org/diseases-conditions/narcissistic-personality-disorder/symptoms-causes/syc-20366662

Mayo Clinic (n.d). Self-Esteem Check: Too Low or Just Right? Retrieved from Mayo Clinic: https://www.mayoclinic.org/healthy-lifestyle/adult-health/in-depth/self-esteem/art-20047976

McAllister, D "Moving On: How to Properly Grieve and Heal After a Breakup" The Hope Line Retrieved from https://www.thehopeline.com/how-to-grieve-heal-after-breakup/

McBride, K. (2017, May). How Does a Narcissist Think? Retrieved from Psychology Today: https://www.psychologytoday.com/us/blog/the-legacy-distorted-love/201705/how-does-narcissist-think

Miller, A.M & Lyon, L. (2018, July). 10 Myths About Narcissism. Health US News. Retrieved from:

https://health.usnews.com/wellness/mind/articles/2018-07-23/10-myths-about-narcissism

Milstead, K. (2018, July). 7 Reasons Why Narcissists Won't Give You Closure. Retrieved from Fairy Tale Shadows: https://fairytaleshadows.com/seven-reasons-why-narcissists-wont-give-you-closure/

Milstead, K. (2019, May). How the Narcissistic Abuse Cycle Keeps Us From Leaving. Retrieved from Fairy Tale Shadows: https://fairytaleshadows.com/how-narcissistic-abuse-cycle-keeps-us-from-leaving/

National Institute of Mental Health. Personality Disorders. Retrieved from https://www.nimh.nih.gov/health/statistics/personality-disorders.shtml)

Neuharth, D. (2019, July). 10 Things Not to Do with Narcissists. Retrieved from Psychology Today: https://www.psychologytoday.com/us/blog/narcissism-demystified/201907/10-things-not-do-narcissists

NHS, UK. (n.d). Raising Low Self-Esteem. Retrieved from NHS UK: https://www.nhs.uk/conditions/stress-anxiety-depression/raising-low-self-esteem/

Ni, P. (2017, July). 6 Common Traits of Narcissists and Gaslighters. Retrieved from Psychology Today: https://www.psychologytoday.com/us/blog/communication-success/201707/6-common-traits-narcissists-and-gaslighters

Psychology Today. (n.d). Narcissism. Retrieved from https://www.psychologytoday.com/intl/basics/narcissism

Saeed, K. (2019, April). 7 Signs You're Experiencing Narcissistic Abuse Recovery. Retrieved from Kim Saeed: https://kimsaeed.com/2015/07/13/signs-youve-arrived-survivor-narcissistic-abuse/

Sarkis, S.S (2015, December). 10 Signs You Are in a Relationship with a Narcissist. Retrieved from Psychology Today: https://www.psychologytoday.com/us/blog/here-there-and-everywhere/201512/10-signs-you-are-in-relationship-narcissist

Schneider, A. (2015, March). Idealize, Devalue, Discard: The Dizzying Cycle of Narcissism. Retrieved from GoodTherapy: https://www.goodtherapy.org/blog/idealize-devalue-discard-the-dizzying-cycle-of-narcissism-0325154

Smith, M. & Robinson, L. (2019, December). Narcissistic Personality Disorder. Retrieved from Help Guide:

https://www.helpguide.org/articles/mental-disorders/narcissistic-personality-disorder.htm

Streep, P. (2016, June). Why Recovering From the Narcissist in Your Life Is So Hard. Retrieved from Psychology Today: https://www.psychologytoday.com/intl/blog/tech-support/201606/why-recovering-the-narcissist-in-your-life-is-so-hard

Strong Sensitive Souls "5 Keys to Breaking Bad Relationship Patterns" Retrieved from https://strongsensitivesouls.com/bad-relationship-patterns/

Subramaniam, V (2019) "How to find yourself after a breakup and raise your self-esteem" Mind Body Green Retrieved from https://www.mindbodygreen.com/0-20275/how-to-rebuild-your-sense-of-selfworth-after-a-breakup.html#:~:text=Be%20sure%20to%20take%20care,%2Dcare%20after%20a%20breakup.)

Sullivan, M. (2017, February). Empathy: How It Can Help Us All Right Now. Retrieved from Psychalive: https://www.psychalive.org/empathy-can-help-us-right-now/

The Recovery Village. (2020, January). Narcissistic Personality Disorder. Retrieved from The Recovery Village:

https://www.therecoveryvillage.com/mental-health/narcissistic-personality-disorder/

Whitbourne, S.K. (2016, January). 9 Myths about Narcissism Almost Everyone Believes. Retrieved from Psychology Today: https://www.psychologytoday.com/intl/blog/fulfillment-any-age/201601/9-myths-about-narcissism-almost-everyone-believes

Yates, L. (n.d). How To Know If You Were Dating A Narcissist And How To Recover From It. Retrieved from Letsmend: https://www.letsmend.com/posts/how-to-know-if-you-were-dating-a-narcissist-and-how-to-recover-from-it

Zhu, L (2020) "How to break the cycle of unhealthy relationships" Women Working Retrieved from https://www.womenworking.com/6-ways-to-break-the-cycle-of-unhealthy-relationships/

Printed in Great Britain
by Amazon